ideals Country Bread COOKBOOK

by Darlene Kronschnabel

To most people, the unmistakable aroma of freshly baked bread, piping hot from the oven, brings back memories of childhood days in country kitchens. Don't, however, be content with just memories. Bread baking is easy, it's fun, and it can be a showcase for your creative talents.

Meals can become veritable feasts with bread, warm and fresh from the oven and rolls which are tender, flaky crisp, rich-tasting and heavenly to eat. Also try baking sweet and moist fruit-topped kuchens or irresistible coffee cakes and fruit and nut breads. On those special occasions, bring from the oven breads from other lands, rich with spices and laden with fruit and nuts.

Here, for your pleasure, in the *Ideals Country Bread Cookbook*, is a blending of traditional heirloom recipes, some handed down from generation to generation as well as new ones to share. We are delighted to bring these recipes to you, along with useful baking tips, fascinating tales of bread lore, and our special art and full-color photography. Join us in looking to the past for inspiration. Embellish your bread with love and bake a loaf that will make your grandmother proud.

Darlene Kronschnabel

ISBN 0-89542-608-0

According to legend, early man placed a piece of newly made bread under the stone blade of his plow when cutting the first furrow. He believed this would help the seed bring forth new life.

contents

Editorial Director, James Kuse

Managing Editor, Ralph Luedtke

Production Editor/Manager, Richard Lawson

Photographic Editor, Gerald Koser

Copy Editor, Sharon Style

artwork by
Jim McGath

**photos and layout
designed by**
Marybeth Owens

*Pictured Opposite:
Sesame Potato Twist Loaf, p. 4*

yeast breads

WHITE BATTER BREAD

1 c. milk
3 T. sugar
1 T. salt
2 T. butter or margarine
1 c. warm water
2 pkgs. dry yeast or 2 cakes
  compressed yeast
4¼ c. flour

Scald milk; stir in sugar, salt and butter. Cool to lukewarm. Measure warm water into large bowl. Sprinkle or crumble in yeast; stir until dissolved. Add lukewarm milk mixture. Stir in flour; batter will be fairly stiff. Beat until well blended, about 2 minutes. Cover and let rise in a warm place until more than doubled in bulk, about 40 minutes. Stir batter down. Beat vigorously about ½ minute. Turn into a greased 9¼ x 5¼ x 3-inch loaf pan. Bake in a 375° oven about 50 minutes. Cool on wire rack. Makes 1 loaf.

WHITE BREAD

5½ to 6 c. flour
2 pkgs. dry yeast
1 c. milk
1 c. water
2 T. sugar
2 T. oil
2 t. salt
  Vegetable oil

Stir together 2 cups flour and yeast. In a saucepan, combine milk, water, sugar, oil and salt and heat slowly until warm (120° to 130°). Add liquid ingredients to flour-yeast mixture and beat until smooth, about 3 minutes on high speed of electric mixer. Stir in more flour to make a moderately soft dough. Turn out onto lightly floured surface and knead until smooth and satiny, about 5 to 10 minutes. Cover dough with bowl or pan; let rest 20 minutes. Divide dough into 2 loaves. Place loaves into 2 greased 4½ x 8½-inch pans; brush with oil. Let rise in a warm place until doubled in bulk, about 30 to 45 minutes. Bake in a 400° oven, 35 to 40 minutes. Remove immediately from pans and brush with oil. Cool on wire rack. Makes two 1-pound loaves.

SESAME POTATO TWIST LOAF

½ c. butter
½ c. sieved hot cooked potatoes or
  prepared instant potatoes
2 T. sugar
2 t. salt
1 c. milk, scalded
2 pkgs, dry yeast
⅓ c. warm water
5½ c. flour
1 egg white slightly beaten with 1 T.
  water
  Sesame seeds

In large mixing bowl, add butter to potatoes and stir until melted. Add sugar, salt and milk; stir until mixture is smooth and cooled to lukewarm. Dissolve yeast in warm water; and stir into potato mixture. Stir in 3 cups of the flour, beating with a spoon until smooth. Gradually stir in enough of the remaining flour to make a moderately firm dough which does not stick to sides of bowl. Turn out on a lightly floured board and knead until smooth and elastic, about 10 minutes, working in only as much additional flour as needed (about 1 cup) to prevent dough from sticking. Place dough in a buttered bowl, turning to butter all sides. Cover and let rise in warm place until doubled in bulk, about 50 minutes. Punch dough down and turn out on lightly floured surface. Divide into four parts and roll each part between buttered palms to form a strand about 15 inches long. Spiral-wrap two strands together to form a twisted loaf; tuck ends under. Place into a buttered 9 x 5-inch loaf pan. Repeat with remaining strands. Cover and let rise in a warm place until almost doubled in bulk, about 20 to 30 minutes. Gently brush tops of loaves with egg white mixture, generously sprinkle with sesame seeds. Bake in a 400° oven 10 minutes. Reduce heat to 350° and bake for 35 minutes or until golden brown. Turn loaves out to cool on wire racks. Makes 2 loaves.

While salt adds some flavor to bread, its main purpose is to control the yeast action so that rising will not be too rapid.

GRANDMA'S WHITE BREAD

1 pkg. active dry yeast
¼ c. lukewarm water
2 c. milk, scalded
¼ c. butter or margarine
2 T. sugar
2 t. salt
6 c. flour

Sprinkle yeast into lukewarm water. Let stand for a few minutes; stir to dissolve. Pour hot milk over butter, sugar and salt in large mixing bowl. Cool to lukewarm; add yeast and 3 cups flour. Beat well. Add remaining flour and mix well. Turn out on a floured surface and knead until smooth and satiny, about 8 to 10 minutes. Put in greased bowl, turning once to grease both sides. Cover. Let rise until doubled in bulk, about 1½ hours. Punch down; let rise for 30 minutes. Shape into 2 loaves and put in greased 9 x 5 x 3-inch pans. Let rise until doubled, about 45 minutes. Bake in a 400° oven for about 35 minutes or until brown and sounds hollow when tapped. Makes 2 loaves.

POTATO BREAD

1½ c. mashed potatoes
1½ c. potato water
2 T. sugar
2 T. shortening or butter
2½ t. salt
¼ c. lukewarm water
1 pkg. dry yeast
6½ c. flour

In a saucepan, combine mashed potatoes and potato water. Add sugar, shortening and salt. Stir over low heat until sugar is dissolved. Cool until lukewarm. In large mixing bowl, pour lukewarm water over yeast. Let stand a few minutes; stir until dissolved. Add potato mixture to yeast. Add half of the flour and beat with electric mixer until smooth. Add remaining flour and knead until smooth and satiny. If sticky, add a little more flour. In bowl, knead dough until it leaves the sides of bowl. Grease top, cover with a damp cloth. Let rise in warm place until doubled in bulk. Punch down dough. Divide in half and shape into 2 round loaves or place in greased 9 x 5 x 3-inch loaf pans. Cover with damp cloth and let rise until doubled in bulk. Bake in a 450° oven for 15 minutes. Reduce heat to 350° and bake about 35 minutes more or until golden. Makes 2 loaves.

BREAD GLAZES

Use any one of the following glazes to create different crusts.

SOFT, BUTTERY CRUST

Brush loaves with softened or melted butter or margarine after baking.

CRISP, SHINY CRUST

Brush loaves with a mixture of 1 egg and 1 tablespoon water just before baking. May be sprinkled with poppy or sesame seed.

DELICATESSEN BREAD CRUST

Remove loaves from oven 5 minutes before done. Combine ½ teaspoon cornstarch and ¼ cup water and heat to boiling. Brush loaves with mixture and return to oven to finish baking.

CINNAMON SUGAR CRUST

Brush loaves with 2 tablespoons melted butter or margarine; sprinkle with mixture of 2 tablespoons sugar and ½ teaspoon cinnamon.

SLIGHTLY CRISP AND SHINY, SWEET CRUST

After baking, brush loaves with a mixture of 1 tablespoon each sugar and water.

AUNT MARTHA'S WHITE BREAD

6 to 7 c. flour
2 pkgs. active dry yeast
1 T. salt
1 c. water
1 c. milk, scalded
¼ c. mild-flavored honey
¼ c. vegetable oil
2 eggs

In large bowl of electric mixer, blend together 2½ cups of the flour, yeast and salt. Add water, honey and oil to milk. Cool to lukewarm. Stir into flour mixture. Add eggs; blend at low speed until moistened then beat 3 minutes at medium speed. Beat in remaining flour until mixed. Turn dough out on a lightly floured board. Knead until smooth and elastic (about 5 minutes). Place in greased bowl; turning to grease both sides. Cover and let rise in warm place until doubled in bulk (about 1 hour). Punch down dough, divide in half, and shape into two loaves. Place in greased 9 x 5 x 3-inch loaf pans. Cover and let rise until doubled in bulk (about 30 minutes). Bake in a 375° oven for 35 to 45 minutes. Remove from pans. Cool on wire racks. Makes 2 loaves.

HUNTERS' BREAD

5 to 5½ c. flour
2 pkgs. dry yeast
1 c. milk
1 c. water
½ c. light molasses
2 t. salt
2 T. vegetable oil
1 c. wheat cereal, uncooked
   Vegetable oil

Stir together 2 cups of the flour and yeast. Combine milk, water, molasses, 2 tablespoons oil, and salt. Place over low heat until warm (120° to 130°). Add liquid ingredients to flour-yeast mixture and beat until smooth, about 3 minutes on high speed of electric mixer. Stir in uncooked cereal and beat 1 minute. Let sit about 5 minutes to let cereal absorb moisture. Stir in additional flour, making a moderately soft dough. Turn out onto lightly floured surface and knead until smooth and satiny, about 5 to 10 minutes. Cover dough with bowl and let rest 45 minutes. Divide dough in half and shape into 2 loaves. Place in 2 greased 4½ x 8½-inch loaf pans. Brush with oil. Let rise in a warm place until doubled in bulk, about 1 hour. Bake in a 400° oven 35 to 40 minutes. If necessary, cover with foil the last 15 minutes of baking to prevent excessive browning. Remove immediately from pans and brush with oil. Cool on wire racks. Makes 2 loaves.

WHOLE WHEAT BREAD

2 pkgs. dry yeast
¾ c. warm water
1¼ c. buttermilk
1½ c. flour
3 c. whole wheat flour
¼ c. shortening
2 T. sugar
2 t. baking powder
2 t. salt
   Softened butter or margarine

Dissolve yeast in warm water in a large mixer bowl. Add buttermilk, 1½ cups flour, 1 cup of the whole wheat flour, the shortening, sugar, baking powder and salt. Blend 30 seconds on low speed, scraping bowl constantly. Beat 2 minutes on medium speed, occasionally scraping bowl. Stir in remaining whole wheat flour. (Dough should remain soft and slightly sticky.) Turn dough onto well-floured board; knead 5

minutes, or about 200 turns. Roll dough into an 18 x 9-inch rectangle. Roll up, beginning at short side. With side of hand, press each end to seal. Fold ends under loaf. Place seam side down in a greased 9 x 5 x 3-inch loaf pan. Brush loaf lightly with butter. Let rise in warm place until doubled in bulk, about 1 hour. Center should rise about 2 inches above pan. Bake on lower rack in a 425° oven 30 to 35 minutes. Remove from pan. Brush with butter; cool on wire rack. Makes 1 loaf.

Your bread recipe reads: "knead until smooth and satiny." How long is that? Most doughs require from 8 to 10 minutes of kneading before you recognize a smooth and satiny surface. After 10 minutes, grasp your dough in one hand, squeezing in slightly with your fingers. If fully developed, the opposite side of the dough ball should feel smooth and taut. You will also see bubbly blisters under the surface.

CRACKED WHEAT BREAD

2 pkgs. dry yeast
¼ c. lukewarm water
4 c. milk, scalded
⅓ c. honey
4 t. salt
6 T. butter
4½ to 5 c. cracked wheat flour
7 to 8 c. white flour

Soften yeast in lukewarm water. Set aside. Pour scalded milk into large mixing bowl. Add honey, butter and salt. Cool to lukewarm. Add yeast mixture and 2 cups cracked wheat flour, stirring to make a batter. Beat thoroughly. Combine remaining cracked wheat flour with 7 cups white flour. Add to batter. Turn out on a floured surface and knead about 10 to 12 minutes or until a smooth satiny ball is formed. Place in a greased bowl. Cover and let rise in a warm place until doubled in bulk. Knead down slightly without adding more flour; cover and let rise again until doubled. Shape into 4 loaves and place into 4 well-greased 4½ x 8½-inch loaf pans. Brush tops with melted butter. Cover and let rise until doubled in size. Bake in a 400° oven 30 to 35 minutes or until golden brown. Makes 4 loaves.

Pictured Opposite:
Hunters' Bread

OATMEAL-WHEAT BREAD

2 c. whole wheat flour
¼ c. instant mashed potato granules
3 pkgs. dry yeast
1 T. salt
2 c. milk
⅓ c. honey
¼ c. butter
½ c. uncooked rolled oats
2½ to 3 c. flour

Combine whole wheat flour, potato granules, yeast and salt in a large bowl. Heat milk, honey and butter until lukewarm; add to flour mixture. Beat at low speed of electric mixer 30 seconds, scraping bowl frequently. Beat 3 minutes at medium speed. Stir in oats and enough flour to make a stiff dough. Knead on floured surface until smooth and elastic, 7 to 10 minutes. Place in a greased bowl, turning to grease all surfaces. Cover and let rise in warm place until doubled in bulk, 1 to 1½ hours. Punch down, divide in half, cover and let dough rest 10 minutes. On a floured surface, roll out each half to a 12 x 7-inch rectangle. Starting with 7-inch side, roll up tightly, jelly-roll fashion. Seal seam and ends. Place seam side down in 2 well-greased 9 x 5 x 3-inch pans. Cover and let rise again until doubled in bulk, 45 to 60 minutes. Bake in a 375° oven for 35 to 40 minutes, until deep golden brown. Remove from pan and cool. Makes 2 loaves.

SWISS WHEAT BREAD

2 c. whole wheat flour
¾ c. flour
1 T. baking powder
1½ t. salt
1 t. baking soda
2 eggs, beaten
1½ c. milk
⅓ c. vegetable oil
¼ c. light brown sugar, firmly packed
1 T. instant minced onion
1 c. shredded Swiss cheese

Stir together flours, baking powder, salt and soda. Set aside. Combine eggs, milk, oil, sugar and onion; stir in Swiss cheese. Add liquid ingredients all at once to flour mixture, stirring only until flour is moistened. Turn into a greased and floured 4½ x 8½-inch loaf pan. Bake in a 375° oven 50 to 55 minutes, or until cake tester comes out clean. If necessary, cover for the last few

minutes to prevent excess browning. Cool in pan on wire rack 10 minutes before removing to cool completely. Makes 1 loaf.

It is possible to knead dough too much. When the dough is smooth and elastic and little bubbles can be seen beneath the surface, it is time to stop. If kneading is continued the dough tears and becomes sticky again. The sticky dough makes a poor quality bread because the gluten has broken down.

DILL PICKLE RYE

4 c. flour
2 c. rye flour
2 pkgs. dry yeast
½ c. boiling water
2 t. dill seed
½ c. water
½ c. liquid from jar of Polish-style pickles
½ c. buttermilk
2 T. sugar
2 T. oil
2 t. salt
2 t. caraway seed
Oil *or* 1 egg, beaten

Combine flours. Stir together 2 cups of the flour with yeast. Heat ½ cup of the water to boiling. Pour over dill seed and soak about 10 minutes; do not drain. In a saucepan, combine ½ cup water, pickle juice, buttermilk, sugar, oil and salt; heat slowly until warm. Stir in dill seed, including water, and caraway seed. Add to flour-yeast mixture and beat until smooth, about 3 minutes on high speed of electric mixer. Stir in remaining flour to make a soft dough. Turn out onto lightly floured surface and gently knead until smooth, about 5 to 8 minutes. Cover dough with bowl or pan and let rest 40 minutes. While dough is resting, grease two 1-quart round glass casseroles. Divide dough in half and shape into balls; place in greased casseroles. Cut three slits in top of each loaf with a sharp knife. For a soft crust, brush top with oil. For a shiny, firm crust, brush with beaten egg. Let rise in warm place about 40 minutes until doubled in bulk. Bake in a 350° oven 50 to 55 minutes or until bread sounds hollow when lightly tapped. Cover tops with foil the last 10 minutes of baking to prevent excessive browning. Makes 2 loaves.

PUMPERNICKEL BREAD

4 c. white flour
2 c. rye flour
½ c. cornmeal
1 T. salt
1 pkg. dry yeast
2 c. water
¼ c. molasses
1 1-oz. sq. unsweetened chocolate
1 T. butter
1 c. mashed potatoes
1 t. caraway seed (optional)

Combine white flour and rye flour. Mix 1½ cups of the mixed flours in a large bowl with cornmeal, salt and yeast. In a saucepan, combine water, molasses, chocolate and butter and heat until very warm (120° to 130°), stirring occasionally. Cool slightly. Gradually add liquids to flour and yeast, beating thoroughly. Add mashed potatoes, 1 cup of the mixed flours and caraway seed; beat 2 minutes on medium speed of electric mixer. Beat in as much remaining flour as possible; continue to gradually add flour, kneading 8 to 10 minutes. Place dough in a large greased bowl, cover and let rise in a warm place until doubled in bulk, about 1 hour. Punch down and let rise again, about 30 minutes. Divide dough in half and shape into two round loaves; place on greased baking sheets. Cover and let rise until doubled in bulk, 30 to 45 minutes. Bake in a 350° oven 45 minutes. Makes 2 round loaves.

CARAWAY RYE BREAD

2½ c. rye flour
2½ c. flour
1 pkg. dry yeast
2 T. caraway seed
1 T. salt
1 t. anise seed, lightly crushed
1¾ c. water
3 T. molasses or honey
¼ c. butter or margarine
1 egg white, lightly beaten

Combine flours, yeast, caraway seed, salt and anise seed and set aside. In a saucepan combine water, molasses and butter; heat just until warm (butter does not need to melt). In large bowl of an electric mixer, combine 2½ cups of the flour mixture with the warm liquid. Beat at medium speed 2 minutes. Add ½ cup more flour mixture or enough to make a thick batter. Beat at high speed 2 minutes. With spoon, stir in remaining flour, or enough to make a soft dough. Turn onto a lightly floured board and knead for about 8 minutes or until dough is smooth and elastic. Place in lightly floured bowl; cover and let rise in warm place 1 hour or until doubled in bulk. Punch dough down. On a floured board knead lightly. Divide in two; shape each into a round bread. Place on greased and floured baking sheet. Cover and let rise 1 hour or until doubled in bulk. Brush with egg white. If desired, sprinkle with more caraway seed. Bake in a 400° oven about 25 minutes or until bread sounds hollow when tapped on the bottom. Cool on wire racks. Makes 2 loaves.

GRANARY BREAD

3½ to 4½ c. all-purpose flour
2 pkgs. dry yeast
1 T. salt
⅓ c. honey
3 T. butter or margarine
2½ c. hot tap water
2½ c. graham flour
Vegetable oil

Combine 2 cups all-purpose flour, undissolved yeast and salt in a large bowl. Stir well to blend. Add honey and butter; stir in hot tap water. Beat with electric mixer at medium speed for 2 minutes, scraping bowl occasionally. Add 1 cup all-purpose flour and ½ cup graham flour. Beat with electric mixer at high speed for 1 minute or until thick and elastic. Stir in remaining graham flour with a wooden spoon; gradually stir in just enough of the remaining all-purpose flour to make a soft dough which leaves sides of bowl. Turn out onto floured board. Knead 5 to 10 minutes or until dough is smooth and elastic. Cover with plastic wrap, then a towel. Let rest 20 minutes. Punch dough down and divide in half. Shape each half into a round loaf about 8 inches in diameter. Flatten slightly. Place in 2 greased 8-inch pie pans or at opposite ends of a greased baking sheet. Brush dough lightly with oil. Cover pans loosely with plastic wrap. Refrigerate 2 to 24 hours. When ready to bake, remove from refrigerator and uncover. Let stand 10 minutes while preheating oven. Cut six ¼-inch deep slashes, spoke fashion, in tops of loaves just before baking. Curve slashes slightly from center to edges of loaves. Bake in a 400° oven 30 to 40 minutes or until done. Remove from pan immediately. Cool on rack. Makes 2 loaves.

GOLDEN HONEY BREAD

5½ to 6½ c. flour
2 pkgs. active dry yeast
1 T. salt
2¼ c. hot tap water
¼ c. honey
¼ c. softened butter or margarine
Vegetable oil

In a large mixing bowl, combine 2 cups of the flour, yeast and salt. Add hot water, honey and butter. Beat with electric mixer at medium speed, 2 minutes, scraping bowl. Add 1 cup flour; beat at high speed for 1 minute or until dough is thick and elastic. Using wooden spoon, gradually stir in enough of the remaining flour to make a soft dough that leaves sides of bowl. Turn out onto floured board. Knead until smooth and elastic (5 to 10 minutes). Cover with plastic wrap then a towel and let rest 20 minutes. Punch dough down. Divide dough in half and shape into loaves. Place in greased 8½ x 4½ x 2½-inch loaf pans. Brush dough lightly with oil. Cover pans loosely with plastic wrap. Refrigerate 2 to 24 hours. When ready to bake, remove from refrigerator. Uncover and let stand 10 minutes. Bake in a 400° oven 30 to 40 minutes or until done. Remove from pans immediately. Brush top crusts with butter, if desired. Complete cooling on racks. Makes 2 loaves.

Note: Unsifted whole wheat flour may be used. Bread will be more compact.

ANADAMA BATTER BREAD

2 pkgs. dry yeast *or* 2 cakes
    compressed yeast
½ c. lukewarm water
1½ c. enriched cornmeal
⅓ c. molasses
¼ c. shortening
1 T. salt
2 c. boiling water
4 c. flour

Dissolve yeast in lukewarm water (warm water for dry yeast). Combine cornmeal, molasses, shortening and salt in large bowl. Stir in boiling water; cool to lukewarm. Beat in 1 cup of the flour. Stir in yeast mixture. Add 2 cups flour, beating 2 minutes on medium speed of electric mixer or 300 vigorous strokes with a wooden spoon. Beat in remaining 1 cup flour with spoon. (Batter will be sticky.) Spoon into 2 greased 4½ x 8½ x 2-inch loaf pans. Spread batter evenly with a greased spatula or knife. Cover and let rise in warm place until doubled in bulk, or about 45 minutes. Bake in a 375° oven 50 minutes. Remove from pans immediately. Brush tops lightly with melted butter if desired. Cool. Makes 2 loaves.

> Never add chilled ingredients to a yeast bread mixture. Use them only after they have reached room temperature, speeding rising time.

RAISIN CINNAMON BREAD

1⅓ c. lukewarm milk
1 pkg. dry yeast
½ c. sugar
1 egg
¼ t. salt
½ c. melted butter
4 c. flour
1 t. cardamom
1 c. raisins or currants
2 T. sugar mixed with 2 T. cinnamon
1 egg white, lightly beaten

Dissolve dry yeast in 1/3 cup of the lukewarm milk and set aside. Combine remaining milk, sugar, egg, salt and butter. Sift cardamom with flour and add a little to the milk mixture, beating until smooth. Add yeast mixture and remaining flour mixture and beat until dough is firm and smooth. Let rise in a warm place until doubled in bulk. Roll dough out, keeping it about 9 inches wide, and sprinkle with raisins and cinnamon mixture. Roll like a jelly roll, tucking ends under. Place in a greased 9 x 5 x 3-inch loaf pan. Cover and let rise 35 minutes. Brush bread with egg white. Slash top and bake in a 375° oven 40 minutes or until golden. Makes 1 loaf.

MINIATURE RAISIN CINNAMON SNAILS

Make up one batch of dough for Raisin Cinnamon Bread. Proceed as directed for rolling up like jelly roll, making the roll 1½ inches in diameter. Cut roll in ½-inch slices and place on greased cookie sheets. Brush with lightly beaten egg white and sprinkle with sugar. Let rise in a warm place until doubled in bulk. Bake in a 375° oven for 20 to 25 minutes until golden. Makes 2 dozen snails.

Pictured Opposite:
Raisin Cinnamon Bread

NATURE BREAD

2 pkgs. dry yeast
¼ c. warm water
2 c. milk, made from nonfat dry milk
⅓ c. softened butter
1 c. wheat germ
1 c. toasted sesame seeds
1 c. raisins
¾ c. shredded carrot
3 T. sugar
2½ t. salt
⅓ c. molasses
2½ to 3 c. whole wheat flour
2½ to 3 c. white flour
Melted butter or oil

Dissolve yeast in warm water and set aside. Scald milk, combine in large mixer bowl with butter. After butter melts, stir in wheat germ, sesame seed, raisins, carrot, sugar, salt and molasses. Cool to lukewarm. Stir in yeast. Combine 1½ cups each of whole wheat flour and white flour; stir into milk mixture, beating well. Stir in remaining flours, a little at a time, using equal amounts of each. Stir until dough leaves sides of the bowl. Knead on lightly floured board until smooth and elastic, about 10 minutes. Place in a greased bowl. Turn to grease top or brush with melted butter or oil. Cover and let rise in warm place until doubled in bulk, about 1 to 1½ hours. Dough will be heavy. Punch down. Divide dough in half; roll each half to a 12 x 8-inch rectangle. Roll up tightly, starting with short side; seal and tuck ends under. Place each loaf in a 8½ x 2½-inch loaf pan. Cover and let rise in a warm place until doubled in bulk, about 1½ to 2 hours. Bake in a 375° oven 45 minutes, covering tops of loaves with foil after 15 minutes to prevent excess browning. When done, remove from pans and cool on racks. Bread slices best when cool and freezes well. Makes 2 very heavy loaves.

INJUN PUDDIN' BREAD

2 pkgs. dry yeast
½ c. warm water
1½ c. water
1 c. yellow cornmeal
⅓ c. vegetable oil
½ c. dark molasses
4 t. salt
2 eggs
5½ c. flour
Cornmeal and salt
Topping

In a bowl dissolve yeast in ½ cup water. Stir in remaining water, cornmeal, oil, molasses, salt, eggs and 2¾ cups of the flour. Beat 1 minute on medium speed of mixer or 300 strokes by hand. Scrape sides and bottom of bowl frequently. Blend in remaining flour with spoon until smooth. Spread batter in a greased 10-inch tube pan; pat into shape with floured hand. Let rise until doubled in bulk, about 1 hour. Sprinkle loaf with a little cornmeal and salt. Bake in a 375° oven 50 to 55 minutes. Serve warm as bread or, if desired, serve with Topping and ice cream for dessert. Makes one 10-inch round loaf.

TOPPING

1 T. molasses
1 c. corn syrup
2 T. butter or margarine

Combine ingredients and heat until warm.

PIONEER BREAD

1 c. cornmeal
1½ T. salt
⅔ c. dark molasses
½ c. vegetable oil
2 c. boiling water
4 pkgs. dry yeast
1 c. warm water
2 c. whole wheat flour
1½ c. rye flour
¼ c. sesame seed
About 5 to 6 cups unbleached flour

In a large bowl, combine cornmeal, salt, molasses, oil and boiling water. Let stand until lukewarm, about ½ hour. Dissolve yeast in the warm water; let stand 10 minutes. Stir into cornmeal mixture. Add whole wheat flour, rye flour and sesame seed; combine at low speed on electric mixer. Beat at high speed for 3 minutes. By hand, add enough unbleached flour to make a soft dough which will leave the sides of the bowl. (Dough will be sticky.) Turn out onto a floured surface; knead 10 minutes, adding more unbleached flour as needed. Place dough in a large greased bowl, turning to grease top of dough. Cover and let rise until doubled in bulk, about 1 to 1½ hours. Punch down dough; turn out on floured surface and divide into 4 parts. Shape each quarter into a loaf; place in a greased 8½ x 4½ x 3-inch bread pan. Cover and let rise until doubled in bulk, 45 to 60 minutes. Bake in a 375° oven 35 to 40 minutes. Makes 4 loaves.

POTATO CHEESE LOAVES

1 c. milk
2 T. softened butter
2 pkgs. dry yeast
1½ c. warm water
2 T. sugar
2 T. prepared yellow mustard
1½ t. salt
¼ c. mashed potato granules
2 c. shredded Cheddar or American cheese
6 to 7 c. flour
1 egg, slightly beaten
Seasame or poppy seed

Heat milk and butter to scalding; cool to lukewarm. In a large bowl, dissolve yeast in warm water. Add cooled milk, sugar, mustard and salt. Stir in potato granules, cheese and enough flour to make a soft dough. Knead on floured surface about 8 to 10 minutes until smooth and satiny. Place in greased bowl; cover and let rise in warm place until light and doubled in bulk, 45 to 60 minutes. Punch down, divide in half and shape into 2 loaves. Place in 2 well-greased 9 x 5-inch loaf pans. Brush with beaten egg; sprinkle with sesame seed. Let rise again until doubled in size, 30 to 45 minutes. Bake in a 375° oven, 45 to 50 minutes, until deep golden brown. Makes 2 loaves.

CASSEROLE GARLIC BREAD

1 c. milk, scalded
2 pkgs. dry yeast
1 c. lukewarm water
2 T. sugar
2 T. butter
2 t. garlic salt
4 to 4½ c. flour
1 egg white, slightly beaten with 1 T. water
Sesame seed

Scald milk and cool to lukewarm. Soften yeast in lukewarm water. In large mixer bowl, combine sugar, butter, garlic salt and 2 cups flour. Add cooled milk and softened yeast to dry ingredients. Blend at low speed until ingredients are mixed, then increase to medium speed and beat for 2 minutes. Stir in remaining flour by hand, blending well. Cover bowl with a damp cloth. Let dough rise in a warm place 30 minutes or until doubled in bulk. Beat down for 1 minute. Turn dough into a well-greased 1½-quart round baking pan or casserole. Combine egg white and water, whip together slightly. Brush top of dough with mixture. Sprinkle

with sesame seeds. Bake in a 375° oven 55 to 60 minutes or until golden brown. Cover with foil to prevent excessive browning. Cool several minutes before removing from pan. Serve warm. Makes 1 loaf.

> After kneading yeast bread dough, the mixture needs to rise until doubled in bulk, a time lapse usually of between one and one-half to two hours. If you're not sure whether leavening is complete, gently press a finger in the dough. A not-yet-ready product will resist pressure; but your finger will leave an impression in a fully-leavened dough.

CHEESE BREAD

5 to 6 c. flour
2 pkgs. dry yeast
2 T. sugar
2 t. salt
1 t. dry mustard
Dash cayenne
1 12-oz. can beer or 1½ c. milk
½ c. water
1 8-oz. pkg. American process cheese, cubed
2 T. butter
1 T. Worcestershire sauce
Vegetable oil

Stir together 2 cups flour, yeast, sugar, salt, mustard and cayenne. Heat beer, water, cheese and butter over low heat to melt most of cheese. Cool to lukewarm. Add liquid ingredients to flour-yeast mixture and beat until smooth, about 3 minutes. Stir in Worcestershire sauce and add enough flour to make a soft dough. Turn out onto a floured surface and knead until smooth and satiny, about 5 to 8 minutes. Place dough in greased bowl, turning to grease top. Cover and let rise in warm place until doubled in bulk, about 45 to 60 minutes. Punch down dough. Divide in two parts. Roll each half to a 5 x 11-inch rectangle. Cut each rectangle into 3 long strips, leaving strips joined at one end and braid. Place in 2 greased 5 x 9-inch loaf pans. Brush with oil. Let rise in warm place until doubled in bulk, 45 to 60 minutes. Bake in a 350° oven 45 to 55 minutes or until deep golden brown. Cover with foil if browning too quickly. Remove from pans immediately. Cool on wire racks. Makes 2 loaves.

ORANGE OATMEAL BREAD

1 pkg. dry yeast
¼ c. warm water
2 c. milk
2 c. uncooked oats, regular or
  quick-cooking
¼ c. butter
2 c. orange juice
½ c. molasses
1 T. salt
⅔ c. sugar
2 c. raisins
10 c. flour

In a small cup, sprinkle yeast over warm water; stir until dissolved and set aside. Scald milk; pour over oats and butter in a large mixing bowl. Let stand 30 minutes. Add orange juice, molasses, salt, sugar, raisins and dissolved yeast mixture to oats. Stir in enough flour to make a soft dough. Place in a greased bowl; cover and let rise until doubled in bulk, about 1½ hours. Turn out onto a floured surface and knead 10 minutes. Shape into 3 loaves and place in 3 greased 9 x 5 x 3-inch loaf pans. Cover and let rise until doubled in bulk, 1½ to 2 hours. Bake in a 350° oven 1 hour, or until loaves sound hollow when tapped on top. Cool. Makes 3 loaves.

ENGLISH MUFFIN BREAD

3 to 4 c. flour
2 pkgs. dry yeast
¼ c. sugar
2 t. salt
1¼ c. hot tap water
½ c. vegetable oil
2 eggs
  Enriched cornmeal

In a large bowl, combine 1½ cups of the flour, yeast, sugar and salt. Add hot water and mix until dry ingredients are moistened. Beat until smooth, about 2 minutes on medium speed of electric mixer. Blend in oil and eggs. Add more flour to make a stiff batter. Beat until batter is smooth and elastic, about 1 minute on medium speed. Cover and let rise in warm place until light and bubbly, about 1 hour. Stir down. Grease 2 4½ x 8½-inch loaf pans and dust with cornmeal. Divide dough and place half in each pan. Cover and let rise in warm place until doubled in bulk, about 30 minutes. Bake in a 375° oven 15 to 20 minutes. Let cool completely in pans. To serve, slice and toast. Makes 2 loaves.

Pictured Opposite:
Crusty Breadsticks, p. 20

ALMOND RAISIN BREAD

1 pkg. dry yeast
¼ c. warm water
1¼ c. milk, scalded
¾ c. butter
½ c. sugar
1 t. salt
2 eggs
4 c. flour
½ c. blanched whole almonds
½ c. white seedless raisins
  Confectioners' sugar

Dissolve yeast in warm water. Scald milk; add butter, sugar and salt. Let cool and add yeast softened in warm water. Beat in eggs, one at a time. Beat well after each addition. Add flour one cup at a time, beating well after each addition. Stir in raisins. Cover and let rise in a warm place until doubled in bulk. Generously grease a fluted tube pan with butter or margarine. Fasten almonds to sides of pan with butter. Pour dough into pan. Let rise until doubled in bulk. Bake in a 350° oven about 50 minutes. Loosen with a plastic spatula, invert and tip out on a wire rack. Sprinkle with confectioners' sugar. Makes 1 loaf.

HONEY OATMEAL CASSEROLE BREAD

3 to 3½ c. flour
2 pkgs. dry yeast
1 c. water
½ c. butter
¼ c. honey
2 t. salt
2 eggs
1 c. quick-cooking oats
  Melted butter

Stir yeast into 1¼ cups of the flour. In a saucepan, combine water, butter, honey and salt and heat slowly until warm. Cool slightly. Add to flour-yeast mixture and beat until smooth, about 1 minute on medium speed of electric mixer. Beat in eggs and oats. Stir in enough additional flour to make a stiff batter. Beat until batter is smooth and elastic, about 1 minute on medium speed. Cover and let rise in warm place until light and bubbly, about 1 hour. Stir down and turn into a well-greased 2-quart casserole dish. Bake at once in a 375° oven 45 to 50 minutes or until golden brown and bread begins to shrink from sides of dish. Cool on wire rack 10 minutes before removing from dish. Brush with melted butter. Makes one 2-quart loaf.

rolls and breadsticks

ONION SURPRISE BUNS

3½ to 4½ c. flour
1 c. rye flour
2 pkgs. dry yeast
1 c. milk
1 c. water
¼ c. light brown sugar, firmly packed
2 t. salt
2 T. vegetable oil
1 1⅜-oz. pkg. dry onion soup mix
¼ c. butter, softened
1 egg, beaten
Caraway seed

Stir together 1 cup flour, rye flour and yeast. Heat milk, water, sugar, salt and oil over low heat until very warm, stirring to blend. Add liquid ingredients to flour mixture and beat until smooth, about 2 minutes, on high speed of electric mixer. Stir in more flour to make a moderately stiff dough. Turn onto lightly floured surface and knead until smooth and satiny, about 8 to 10 minutes. Cover with bowl and let rest 45 minutes. During rest period, grease two baking sheets. Divide dough in half; shape into balls. Roll each half into a 12 x 12-inch square; cut into 3 x 4-inch rectangles. Combine soup mix and butter. Spread mixture over lengthwise center third of each rectangle. Fold outside portions lengthwise over center third. Seal bottom and edges securely. Place on greased baking sheets. Brush with egg and sprinkle with caraway seed. Let rise in warm place until doubled in bulk about 45 minutes. Bake in a 400° oven 12 to 15 minutes. Remove from baking sheets immediately. Makes 2 dozen buns.

POTATO REFRIGERATOR ROLLS

1 pkg. dry yeast
1½ c. lukewarm potato water
⅔ c. butter
⅔ c. sugar
1½ t. salt
1 c. sieved lukewarm potatoes
4 egg yolks plus 2 tablespoons water
7 c. flour (about)

Dissolve yeast in ¼ cup of the potato water. In a large bowl, cream butter, sugar and salt.

Blend in sieved potatoes. Add remaining water and beaten egg yolks to which yeast mixture has been added. Add about 3 cups of the flour and beat thoroughly. Continue to add and stir in remaining flour until dough does not stick to the bowl. Turn out on a floured board and knead about 5 minutes or until dough holds a smooth shape. Place in a greased bowl and cover. Let rise for 2 hours. Punch down and let rise for another 45 minutes. Punch down, turn onto floured board. Shape into 2-inch balls and flatten slightly. Place in a greased 15 x 9-inch pan. Let rise in a warm place until doubled in bulk. Bake in a 400° oven 15 to 18 minutes or until golden brown. Makes 18 rolls.

POPPY SEED ROLLS

1 cake compressed yeast
¼ c. lukewarm water
¾ c. milk
3 T. sugar
3 T. shortening
¾ t. salt
2¾ to 3 c. flour
2 egg yolks, separated
2 T. melted butter
3 T. poppy seed
1 T. cold water

Dissolve yeast in lukewarm water and set aside. Scald milk in a large bowl, add milk to sugar, shortening, and salt. Cool to lukewarm. Add yeast to cooled mixture. Stir in 1 cup flour and beat thoroughly. Allow to rise until doubled in bulk. Add 1 egg yolk and just enough flour to knead, about 1¾ cups. Knead; cover and allow to rise until doubled in bulk. Roll into a round about ¼-inch thick. Spread with melted butter and sprinkle with poppy seed. Cut in triangles, cutting from center to outer edge. Roll each triangle, beginning from outer edge. Place rolls about 3 inches apart on a greased baking sheet. Brush with mixture of beaten egg yolk mixed with 1 tablespoon water. Sprinkle tops with additional poppy seed. Bake in a 400° oven 15 to 20 minutes or until brown. Makes about 1½ dozen rolls.

LUNCHEON ROLLS

4½ to 5 c. flour
2 pkgs. dry yeast
¾ c. milk
½ c. water
¼ c. vegetable oil
¼ c. sugar
2 t. salt
2 eggs, room temperature
Melted butter

Stir together 2 cups flour and yeast. Combine milk, water, oil, sugar and salt in a saucepan and heat until warm (120° to 130°). Add liquid ingredients to flour-yeast mixture and beat until smooth, about 2 minutes on medium speed of electric mixer or 300 strokes by hand. Blend in eggs. Add 1 cup flour and beat 1 minute on medium speed of mixer or 150 strokes by hand. Stir in 1½ to 2 cups additional flour, making a soft dough. Turn onto lightly floured surface and knead until smooth and satiny, 8 to 10 minutes. Cover with bowl and let rest 20 minutes. Shape dough into Ribbon Rolls or Quick Dinner Rolls. Place on greased baking sheet or greased muffin pans. Let rise until doubled, about 30 minutes. Bake in a 400° oven, 15 to 20 minutes or until golden brown. Remove from pans immediately and brush with butter. Makes 24 rolls.

RIBBON ROLLS

Divide dough in half. Cut each portion into 12 equal pieces. Shape into balls; place in greased muffin pans. With scissors, make 3 parallel cuts in each roll, cutting almost to the bottom and forming 4 sections.

QUICK DINNER ROLLS

Divide dough in half. Roll out one portion to a 9 x 12-inch rectangle; brush with butter. With sharp knife, cut rectangle into twelve 3-inch squares. Fold squares in half to form rectangles and seal edges. Place rolls 1 inch apart on greased baking sheet. Repeat for second portion of dough.

Here's an easy way to warm and freshen rolls. Place two to three tablespoons water in a skillet. Place a rack in the pan and arrange rolls on top. Cover skillet and warm rolls over low heat about 10 minutes.

STICKY BUNS

1 c. warm water
1 pkg. dry yeast
1 c. lukewarm milk (scalded then cooled)
3 T. corn oil
2 T. sugar
2 t. salt
2 eggs, beaten
6 c. flour (approximate)
1 c. butter or margarine
⅔ c. dark brown sugar, firmly packed
1½ c. chopped pecans
4 T. melted butter or margarine
2 t. cinnamon
1 c. dark corn syrup

In a large warm mixing bowl, dissolve yeast in warm water. Stir in milk, corn oil, sugar, salt and eggs. Add 3 cups of the flour; beat until smooth. Stir in enough remaining flour to make dough easy to handle. Turn dough onto lightly floured board. Knead until smooth and elastic, about 5 minutes. Place in a greased bowl; turn greased side up. Cover with clean towel and let rise in warm place, free from draft, 1 to 1½ hours or until doubled in bulk. While dough is rising, stir together 1 cup butter and brown sugar. Divide mixture between two 13 x 9 x 2-inch pans, spreading evenly. Sprinkle ¾ cup pecans over mixture in each pan. When dough is doubled, punch down and divide in half. Roll out each half on a lightly floured board to a 15 x 8-inch rectangle. Brush each rectangle with 2 tablespoons melted butter and sprinkle with 1 teaspoon cinnamon. Roll rectangles up jelly-roll fashion beginning at wide side. Pinch edges of dough together along length of roll to seal. Cut each roll into 15 slices. In each pan, arrange 15 slices slightly apart, cut-side up. Cover and let rise 30 minutes or until doubled in bulk. Bake in a 400° oven 20 minutes. Pour ½ cup corn syrup over each pan and bake 5 minutes longer. Remove from oven and let stand 1 minute; invert pans onto large tray. Serve warm. Makes 30 rolls.

BUBBLE BUNS

Prepare dough for Sticky Buns. Omit melted butter and stir the cinnamon into the butter-brown sugar mixture. After dough has risen first time, punch down and divide into quarters. Shape 10 balls from each quarter. Arrange 20 balls in each prepared pan. Cover and let rise; bake as directed. Makes 40 bubble-shaped buns.

YUM-YUM PECAN ROLLS

¾ c. milk, scalded
2 T. sugar
1 t. salt
¼ c. corn oil
1 pkg. dry yeast
¼ c. warm water
1 egg, well beaten
3½ c. flour (about)
3 T. butter or margarine, softened
¼ c. brown sugar, firmly packed
½ c. pecan halves
3 T. butter or margarine, softened
¼ c. brown sugar, firmly packed
2 t. ground cinnamon (optional)
½ c. dark corn syrup

In a small bowl, combine milk, sugar, salt and corn oil; mix well. Cool to lukewarm. In a large bowl, stir yeast into water until dissolved. Add milk mixture and egg. Stir in enough flour to make a stiff dough. Turn dough out onto lightly floured surface; knead until smooth and elastic. Place in a greased bowl, smooth side down. Turn over and cover. Let rise in a warm place about 1½ hours or until doubled in bulk. Spread 3 tablespoons softened butter in a 9 x 9 x 2-inch cake pan. Sprinkle with ¼ cup brown sugar and top with pecan halves. Punch dough down. Place dough on a lightly floured surface; roll into a 12 x 11-inch rectangle, about ¼ inch thick. Spread with remaining butter, brown sugar and cinnamon. Roll up as for a jelly roll, beginning with the 12-inch side. Cut roll into twelve 1-inch slices; place slices cut side down in prepared pan. Pour corn syrup over rolls. Cover and let rise again until doubled in bulk 35 to 40 minutes. Bake in a 425° oven 20 to 25 minutes or until golden brown. Immediately turn out onto large plate. Makes 12 rolls.

CHEESE GARLIC BREADSTICKS

3¼ c. flour
1 pkg. dry yeast
1¼ c. water
1 T. sugar
1 T. vegetable oil
1½ t. salt
1 garlic clove, minced
1 c. grated Parmesan cheese
Water

Stir together 1¼ cups flour and yeast. In a small saucepan, combine water, sugar, oil, salt and garlic, and heat over low heat until warm. Add liquid ingredients to flour-yeast mixture and beat until smooth, about 3 minutes on medium speed of electric mixer or 300 strokes by hand. Add cheese and more flour to make a moderately stiff dough. Turn out onto lightly floured board and knead until smooth and satiny, about 5 minutes. Divide dough into 4 portions. Divide each portion into 10 sections. Roll each section of dough between fingers to form a 9-inch rope. Arrange breadsticks on greased baking sheets, being careful not to stretch. Brush with water. Let rise in a warm place about 45 minutes or until doubled in bulk. Bake in a 400° oven 12 to 15 minutes until lightly brown. Cool. Makes 40 breadsticks.

WALNUT CARAMEL ROLLS

1 pkg. dry yeast
1 c. warm water
¼ c. sugar
1 t. salt
2 T. softened butter
1 egg
3¼ to 3½ c. flour
⅓ c. melted butter
½ c. brown sugar, firmly packed
1 T. dark corn syrup
⅔ c. coarsely chopped walnuts
½ c. sugar
2 t. cinnamon
3 T. melted butter

In a large mixing bowl, dissolve yeast in warm water. Stir in ¼ cup sugar, salt, 2 tablespoons butter, egg and 2 cups of the flour; beat until smooth. Stir in enough remaining flour until dough is easy to handle. Turn by hand several times to shape into a round ball. Place in a greased bowl, turn to grease both sides; cover tightly. Refrigerate overnight. Combine melted butter, brown sugar, corn syrup and chopped walnuts. Pour into a buttered 13 x 9½ x 2-inch pan. Combine remaining sugar and cinnamon. On floured board, roll dough into a 15 x 9-inch rectangle. Spread with melted butter and sprinkle with sugar-cinnamon mixture. Roll up tightly, beginning at wide side. Seal edge well. Cut into 1-inch slices and place in prepared pan. Cover and let rise in warm place until double, about 1½ hours. Bake in a 375° oven 25 to 30 minutes or until golden brown. Makes about 15 rolls.

Pictured Opposite:
Lemon Nut Bread
Applesauce and Raisin Bread
Pumpkin Walnut Bread
all recipes on p. 21

CRUNCHY WHEAT GERM STICKS

1 c. regular wheat germ, divided
½ c. unsifted flour
2 t. chopped chives
¼ t. salt
¼ c. butter
1 egg
2 T. milk, divided

Combine ¾ cup wheat germ, flour, chives and salt in a bowl. Cut in butter until mixture looks like coarse meal. Add egg and 1 tablespoon milk. Stir well with fork. Pinch off pieces of dough and roll into 3½-inch long sticks. Brush with remaining 1 tablespoon milk. Roll in remaining ¼ cup wheat germ. Place on ungreased baking sheet. Bake in a 425° oven about 10 minutes or until golden brown. Makes 1 dozen sticks.

At best, bread baking, in the early days of our country, was hard work. American housewives prepared their own bread starters before compressed yeast was developed in 1868. They carefully preserved the scum from fermenting wine or a mixture of hops and malt. To this they added flour and water to form a starter. Starter could be kept going for years and brides carried the starter as gifts from their mothers into their new homes.

CRUSTY BREADSTICKS

1 pkg. dry yeast
1 c. warm water
3 c. flour
3 T. sugar
1½ t. salt
2 T. shortening
1 egg white, slightly beaten
1 T. water
Coarse salt

In a small bowl, soften yeast in water for 5 minutes. Combine flour, sugar and salt. Cut in shortening with pastry blender or 2 knives until very fine. Add softened yeast and mix until dough is formed. Cover and let dough rest in bowl 20 minutes. Cut off pieces slightly smaller than golf balls. Roll 10 to 12 inches long. Place on greased baking sheet. Let rise uncovered for 20 minutes. Brush with wash made of egg white combined with water. Sprinkle with coarse salt. Bake in a 425° oven 12 to 15 minutes. Makes 2½ dozen.

SNAPPY CHEESE WAFERS

1¼ c. flour
1½ t. baking powder
½ t. salt
2 c. shredded Cheddar cheese
½ c. butter
1 t. Dijon-style mustard
½ t. hot pepper sauce

Stir together flour, baking powder and salt. Combine cheese with remaining ingredients. Work in flour with hands until dough forms a ball. Form into a 12-inch roll and wrap in waxed paper. Chill for 2 hours or overnight. Slice ¼ inch thick and place on an ungreased baking sheet. Bake in a 350° oven 10 to 12 minutes or until lightly browned. Remove immediately from baking sheets and cool on wire rack. Serve plain or with your favorite dip. Makes 4 to 5 dozen wafers. *Note:* Roll may be frozen. Before baking, thaw 10 minutes. Then proceed as directed.

GRAHAM CRACKERS

1 t. baking soda
1 c. milk
1 c. butter or margarine
1 c. sugar
2 eggs, beaten
½ t. salt
5½ to 6 c. graham flour
½ t. baking powder

Dissolve soda in milk and set aside. Cream butter and sugar. Add beaten eggs and mix well. Add soda mixture, graham flour, salt and baking powder. Mixture should resemble a stiff batter, almost stiff enough to roll. Divide into 3 portions. On 3 greased cookie sheets, spread each portion and press smooth to a ¼-inch thickness. Prick with fork. Bake in a 400° oven 12 to 15 minutes. Cut in squares while warm. Cool. Makes about 6 dozen graham crackers.

Creative baking is an art, as inventive as any handicraft. Colonial homemakers perfected the art of baking out of necessity, for it was not until the mid-seventeenth century with the rise of towns and cities, that the baking industry of our young country began.

# fruit and nut breads

PUMPKIN WALNUT BREAD

2 c. flour
2 t. baking powder
½ t. baking soda
1 t. salt
1 t. ground cinnamon
½ t. ground nutmeg
2 eggs
1 c. solid-pack pumpkin
1 c. sugar
½ c. milk
¼ c. melted butter
1 c. chopped walnuts

Sift together first 6 ingredients. Beat eggs slightly in a bowl; stir in pumpkin, sugar, milk and melted butter, mixing well. Add dry ingredients and mix well. Stir in nuts. Spread in a well-greased 9 x 5 x 3-inch loaf pan. Bake in a 350° oven 50 to 55 minutes, or until edges begin to pull away from sides of pan and wooden pick inserted in center comes out clean. Cool in pan on wire rack for 5 minutes, then remove loaf from pan and cool completely. Makes 1 loaf.

LEMON NUT BREAD

2½ c. flour
1 c. sugar
3½ t. baking powder
½ t. baking soda
½ t. salt
½ c. water
⅓ c. melted shortening
2 eggs, beaten
1½ T. freshly grated lemon peel
½ c. freshly squeezed lemon juice
½ c. chopped nuts
½ c. raisins

In a large bowl, sift together dry ingredients. Combine water, shortening, eggs, lemon peel and juice; add to flour mixture. Stir just until blended. Stir in nuts and raisins. Pour into a greased 9 x 5 x 3-inch loaf pan. Bake in a 350° oven for 1 hour and 15 minutes or until toothpick inserted in center comes out clean. Cool 10 minutes; remove from pan. Cool on wire rack. Makes 1 loaf.

APPLESAUCE AND RAISIN BREAD

2 c. flour
1 T. baking powder
1 t. salt
1 t. cinnamon
½ t. ground cloves
1 c. unsweetened applesauce
2 eggs, beaten
¼ c. dark brown sugar, firmly packed
¼ c. vegetable oil
1 c. seedless raisins
½ c. finely chopped nuts (optional)

Stir together flour, baking powder, salt, cinnamon and cloves. Combine applesauce, eggs, sugar and oil; stir in raisins and nuts. Add all at once to flour, stirring only until flour is moistened. Pour into greased 8½ x 4½-inch loaf pan. Bake in a 350° oven 50 to 55 minutes or until done. Allow to cool in pan 15 minutes before removing. Makes 1 loaf.

SWEET POTATO BREAD

2 c. flour
⅓ c. sugar
⅓ c. dark brown sugar, firmly packed
1 T. baking powder
1 t. salt
¼ t. ground allspice
2 eggs, beaten
1 c. mashed cooked sweet potato
½ c. milk
3 T. salad oil
½ c. chopped pecans
6 pecan halves (optional)
1 egg white, beaten (optional)

Stir together flour, sugars, baking powder, salt and allspice. Blend together eggs, sweet potato, milk and oil. Stir in chopped pecans, then add all at once to flour mixture, stirring until blended. Pour into greased 4½ x 8½-inch loaf pan. Bake in a 350° oven 1 hour and 10 minutes. If desired, dip pecan halves into beaten egg white and place on top of loaf for last 10 minutes of baking. Cool on wire rack 10 minutes before removing from pan; cool completely before slicing. Makes 1 loaf.

APRICOT NUT BREAD

1 17-oz. can apricot halves
2 c. flour
1 t. baking powder
½ t. baking soda
½ t. salt
½ c. chopped walnuts
⅔ c. sugar
⅓ c. vegetable shortening
2 eggs
3 T. orange juice

Drain apricots, reserving syrup. Puree apricots in electric blender or force through food mill. Add enough apricot syrup to puree to measure 1 cup. Sift together flour, baking powder, soda and salt; mix with nuts. Cream sugar with shortening; beat in eggs. Stir in orange juice and apricot puree. Add flour-nut mixture and mix well. Pour batter into greased 9 x 5 x 3-inch loaf pan or six greased 4½ x 2½ x 1¼-inch pans. Bake in a 350° oven about 40 to 45 minutes for large loaf, 25 to 30 minutes for small loaves. Cool 10 minutes; remove from pan and cool on rack. Makes 1 large loaf or 6 small ones.

A cooled loaf of homemade bread cuts more neatly than a warm loaf.

ORANGY PUMPKIN BREAD

⅔ c. shortening
2⅔ c. sugar
4 eggs
1 1-lb. can pumpkin
⅔ c. water
3⅓ c. flour
2 t. baking soda
1½ t. salt
1 t. cinnamon
1 t. cloves
½ t. baking powder
1 orange
⅔ c. chopped nuts
⅔ c. chopped raisins or dates

Cream shortening with sugar; add eggs, pumpkin and water. Sift together next 6 ingredients and add to pumpkin mixture. Remove seeds from orange. Using blender or grinder, grind orange, including peel; add to pumpkin batter. Stir in nuts and raisins or dates. Pour into two well-greased 9 x 5 x 3-inch loaf pans or seven 1-pound cans and bake in a 350° oven for 1 hour. Makes 2 large or 7 small loaves.

CHERRY NUT BREAD

4 c. flour
2 t. baking powder
1 t. baking soda
1 t. salt
1¼ c. sugar
⅔ c. shortening
3 eggs
1 17-oz. can applesauce
1 c. chopped nuts
1 16-oz. can red sour pitted cherries, well drained
2 t. cherry extract or almond extract

Sift together flour, baking powder, soda and salt; set aside. Blend sugar and shortening until fluffy. Add eggs and beat until smooth. Add flour mixture, alternating with applesauce. Stir in chopped nuts, drained cherries and cherry extract. Pour into two greased 9 x 5 x 3-inch loaf pans. Bake in a 350° oven 60 to 65 minutes or until an inserted toothpick comes out clean. Remove from pans while warm and when slightly cool spread with vanilla glaze. Makes 2 loaves.

VANILLA GLAZE

1 c. confectioners' sugar
2 T. milk
1 T. butter or margarine
1 t. vanilla

Blend sugar, milk and butter until smooth. Add vanilla and spread on nut bread loaves.

BOSTON BROWN BREAD

1 c. flour
1 c. rye flour
1 c. cornmeal
2 t. baking soda
1 t. salt
½ c. raisins
½ c. chopped nuts
2 c. buttermilk
¾ c. dark molasses

Stir together flours, cornmeal, soda, salt, raisins and nuts. Combine buttermilk and molasses; add all at once to dry mixture. Mix well. Fill 2 well-greased 1-pound molds or coffee cans with batter two-thirds full. Cover molds with double thicknesses of aluminum foil; fasten securely. Put 2 to 3 quarts of water in a large covered pan with rack in bottom. Bring water to a boil. Place molds or cans in pan; reduce heat and steam for 1½ hours. When finished, remove bread from molds immediately. Makes two 1-pound loaves.

Pictured Opposite:
Boston Brown Bread

WHOLE WHEAT FRUIT BREAD

3 c. flour
1 c. whole wheat flour
2 T. baking powder
2 t. baking soda
1 t. salt
1 t. allspice
2 eggs, beaten
1¾ c. milk
1 c. honey
1½ c. chopped, mixed dried fruit

Stir together dry ingredients and set aside. Blend together eggs, milk and honey; stir in dried fruit and add all at once to flour mixture, stirring only until flour is moistened. Pour into 2 well-greased 4½ x 8½-inch loaf pans. Bake in a 350° oven 55 to 65 minutes. If necessary, cover loosely with foil last 20 minutes to prevent excess browning. Cool on wire rack 10 minutes before removing from pans. Cool completely before slicing. Makes 2 loaves.

CRANBERRY BREAD

1½ c. wheat bran flakes
2 c. flour
1½ t. baking powder
½ t. baking soda
½ t. salt
1 c. sugar
½ c. chopped nuts
1 egg
2 T. vegetable oil
1 c. orange juice
1 c. halved cranberries

In a large mixing bowl, combine bran flakes, flour, baking powder, soda, salt, sugar and nuts. Set aside. In a small mixing bowl, beat egg until foamy. Add vegetable oil, orange juice and cranberries, mixing well. Add to dry ingredients, mixing thoroughly. Spread in a well-greased 9 x 5 x 3-inch loaf pan. Bake in a 325° oven about 70 minutes or until wooden toothpick inserted near center comes out clean. Cool 10 minutes; remove from pan. Cool completely on wire rack. Makes 1 loaf.

To freeze homemade breads, prepare and bake as usual. Cool to room temperature, then wrap in moisture-proof material. Baked yeast breads can be stored in the freezer for up to six months.

CARROT BREAD

2 c. flour
2 t. baking soda
2 t. cinnamon
½ t. salt
1½ c. sugar
½ c. dried currants
½ c. flaked coconut
½ c. chopped nuts
1 c. vegetable oil
2 t. vanilla
2 c. grated raw carrot
3 eggs

Mix dry ingredients together. Add currants, coconut and nuts. Add remaining ingredients. Mix well. Pour into a greased 9 x 5 x 3-inch loaf pan. Let stand 20 minutes. Bake in a 350° oven 60 minutes, or until done. Cool in pan 10 minutes. Remove and cool on rack. Makes 1 loaf.

BANANA BROWN BREAD

2 c. whole wheat flour
1 c. yellow cornmeal
¾ t. salt
1 t. baking soda
1 c. mashed ripe banana
   (3 medium bananas)
1 c. buttermilk
¾ c. unsulphured molasses
¾ c. raisins

In a large bowl mix together flour, cornmeal, salt and baking soda. Stir in banana and remaining ingredients. Turn into 3 greased and floured 1-pound cans. Bake in a 350° oven 45 minutes, or until cake tester inserted in center of breads comes out clean. Cool 10 minutes, turn out of cans and serve warm with butter. Loaves may be frozen. Thaw and heat in a 350° oven, wrapped in foil, for 20 minutes. Makes 3 loaves.

ORANGE BLOSSOM PRUNE BREAD

1 c. cooked prunes
2¼ c. flour
1 c. sugar
2½ t. baking powder
¾ t. salt
2 eggs, beaten
3 T. salad oil
1 T. grated orange rind
¾ c. chopped walnuts

Drain prunes, reserving ¾ cup of the liquid. Pit and dice prunes. Sift together flour, sugar, baking powder and salt. Combine eggs, reserved prune liquid, oil and orange rind. Add to dry ingredients, mixing well. Stir in prunes and nuts. Pour into a greased 9 x 5-inch loaf pan. Bake in a 350° oven 1 hour and 10 minutes or until a cake tester inserted in middle comes out clean. Let bread stand 10 minutes. Remove from pan to cool. Makes 1 loaf.

PINEAPPLE ZUCCHINI BREAD

```
3 eggs
2 c. sugar
2 t. vanilla
1 c. salad oil
2 c. zucchini, peeled, grated and drained
3 c. flour
1 t. baking powder
1 t. salt
1 t. baking soda
1 c. crushed pineapple, drained
½ c. seedless raisins
1 c. chopped nuts
```

Beat eggs, sugar, vanilla and oil until fluffy; add zucchini. Combine all dry ingredients and add to egg mixture, mixing well. Stir in pineapple, raisins and nuts. Pour into 2 greased and floured 8½ x 4½-inch loaf pans. Bake in a 325° oven 60 minutes or until bread tests done. Let cool in pans for 10 minutes. Remove and cool completely before slicing. Makes 2 loaves.

WALNUT LEMON BREAD

```
1¼ c. walnuts
 3 c. flour
 ¾ c. sugar
 4 t. baking powder
1½ t. salt
 ¼ t. nutmeg
 1 large egg
1¼ c. milk
 ¼ c. melted butter
 2 t. grated lemon peel
 2 T. lemon juice
```

Chop walnuts coarsely. Sift flour with sugar, baking powder, salt and nutmeg. Beat egg. Add milk, butter, lemon peel and juice. Combine with dry mixture and stir until all of flour is moistened. Stir in 1 cup walnuts. Turn into well-greased 9 x 5 x 2¾-inch loaf pan. Sprinkle with remaining walnuts. Let stand 15 minutes. Bake in a 350° oven for about 60 minutes until loaf tests done. Let stand 10 minutes, then turn out onto wire rack to cool. Makes 1 loaf.

BANANA CURRANT BREAD

```
⅓ c. softened butter or margarine
⅔ c. dark brown sugar, firmly packed
1 t. vanilla
2 eggs
1¾ c. flour
1 t. baking powder
½ t. salt
1 T. lemon juice
1 c. mashed ripe banana
   (3 medium bananas)
½ c. currants
```

In large mixing bowl, cream butter with sugar. Beat in vanilla. Beat in eggs, one at a time. In medium bowl, mix together flour, baking powder and salt; blend into batter alternately with banana and lemon juice. Stir in currants. Turn into 2 greased and floured 1-pound coffee cans. Bake in a 350° oven 60 minutes or until cake tester inserted in center of bread comes out clean. Cool 10 minutes, remove from cans and cool completely. Makes 2 loaves.

Other homemakers used salt-rising methods for bread baking. A mixture of cornmeal, salt, sugar and water was allowed to ferment overnight, and, when combined with other ingredients, produced a tasty bread.

BASIC RAISIN BREAD MIX

```
9 c. flour
1 T. salt
¼ c. baking powder
2 c. vegetable shortening
2 c. raisins
2 c. golden raisins
```

Sift flour, salt and baking powder into large bowl. Cut in shortening to resemble coarse cornmeal. Blend in raisins. Store mixture in a plastic bag in a closed container in refrigerator or in a cool spot on pantry shelf. Makes about 4 quarts.

QUICK RAISIN BREAD

```
3½ c. Basic Raisin Bread Mix
½ c. sugar
¾ c. milk
1 egg, beaten
```

Blend mix with sugar. Combine milk and egg. Mix with dry ingredients just until well blended. Turn into a greased 7 x 2½-inch round baking pan or a 9 x 5-inch loaf pan. Bake in a 350° oven 60 minutes. Makes 1 loaf.

coffee cakes and kuchens

PINEAPPLE-CHERRY COFFEE CAKE

   3 T. softened butter
   3 T. honey
   ⅔ c. crushed pineapple, drained
   6 maraschino cherries, diced
   ¼ c. flaked coconut
   ¾ c. sugar
   ⅓ c. shortening
   2 eggs
2¼ c. flour
   2 t. baking powder
   ½ t. salt
   ¾ c. milk

Combine butter, honey, pineapple, cherries and coconut; set aside. Cream sugar with shortening until fluffy; beat in eggs until light and fluffy. Sift flour, baking powder and salt together; add to egg mixture, alternating with milk and beating smooth after each addition. Pour into a greased and floured 9 x 9 x 2-inch pan. Spread reserved coconut mixture over batter. Bake in a 350° oven 35 to 40 minutes. Cool in pan 10 minutes; remove from pan. Cool on wire rack. When cool, drizzle with Confectioners' Sugar Frosting (page 28).

CRANBERRY COFFEE CAKE

1¼ c. flour
   ½ c. sugar
1½ t. baking powder
   ¼ t. salt
   4 T. butter
   1 egg, slightly beaten
   3 T. milk
   1 t. vanilla
1½ c. chopped fresh cranberries
   ½ c. flour
   ½ c. brown sugar, firmly packed
   ½ t. ground cinnamon
   4 T. butter

Sift together 1¼ cups flour, sugar, baking powder and salt. Cut in 4 tablespoons butter until mixture resembles coarse crumbs. Combine egg, milk and vanilla; add to dry ingredients and mix well. Spread in a greased

8 x 8 x 2-inch baking pan. Spoon cranberries over batter. Combine remaining flour, brown sugar and cinnamon. Cut in remaining butter until mixture resembles coarse crumbs; sprinkle over cranberries. Bake in a 350° oven 45 to 50 minutes or until cake tests done. Serve warm or cold. Makes 1 coffee cake.

RHUBARB KUCHEN

1¾ c. flour
   1 t. baking powder
   2 T. sugar
   ½ t. salt
   ½ c. butter
   ½ c. chopped nuts
   2 egg yolks, beaten
      Filling
      Meringue

Sift together dry ingredients; cut in butter as for pie crust. Add nuts and egg yolks, mixing well. Press in the bottom of a greased 9 x 12-inch baking pan. Make Filling.

FILLING

   2 egg yolks, beaten
   2 c. sugar
   ½ c. flour
   4 to 5 c. rhubarb, cut in 1-inch pieces

Beat egg yolks. Add flour and sugar and blend well. Mix with rhubarb. Pour in crust and bake in a 350° oven 45 minutes. Remove from oven and add Meringue.

MERINGUE

   4 egg whites
   ¼ t. salt
   ¼ t. cream of tartar
   ¾ c. sugar
   1 t. vanilla

Beat egg whites until foamy. Add remaining ingredients and continue to beat until stiff. Cover baked rhubarb and return to oven to bake at 325° for 10 to 12 minutes. Makes 1 large kuchen.

Pictured Opposite:
Rhubarb Kuchen

ALMOND REVEILLE CAKE

1½ c. flour
2 t. baking powder
½ t. baking soda
1 t. salt
1½ c. sugar
½ c. butter
2 eggs
1 c. milk
½ t. almond extract
1 c. rolled oats, quick or old-fashioned
Sliced blanched almonds

Sift together flour, baking powder, soda, salt and sugar into a large bowl. Cut in butter until mixture resembles coarse crumbs. Add eggs, milk and almond extract; mix well. Stir in rolled oats. Pour batter into 2 greased and floured 8-inch round cake pans. Sprinkle with almonds. Bake in a 350° oven about 25 minutes or until golden brown. Cool on wire rack about 5 minutes; remove from pan. Serve warm. Makes two 8-inch coffee cakes.

APPLE KUCHEN

¾ c. sugar
⅓ c. lard
1 egg
1 t. salt
2 t. baking powder
2 c. flour
1 c. milk
1 t. vanilla
3 c. apple slices
¼ c. sugar
1 t. cinnamon
4 T. heavy cream

Cream sugar with lard. Add egg and beat well. Mix together salt, baking powder and flour. Stir into sugar-lard mixture, alternating with milk. Add vanilla and mix well. Pour into a greased 9 x 12 x 2-inch pan. Arrange thick apple slices in neat rows across the top. Stir cinnamon into sugar and sprinkle over apples. Sprinkle heavy cream over the mixture and bake in a 350° oven 30 minutes or until done. Makes 1 kuchen.

CHERRY COFFEE CAKE

3½ to 4½ c. flour
½ c. sugar
1 t. salt
1 pkg. dry yeast
1 c. milk
¼ c. water
½ c. butter
1 egg, at room temperature
½ c. flour
½ c. light brown sugar, firmly packed
½ c. chopped walnuts
¼ t. salt
1 1-lb. can pitted red sour cherries, well drained

In large bowl, with electric mixer, mix 1¼ cups flour, sugar, salt and dry yeast. Set aside. Combine milk, water and butter in a saucepan. Heat over low heat until liquids are warm (120-130°). (Butter need not melt.) Gradually add liquids to dry ingredients and beat two minutes at medium speed of mixer, scraping bowl occasionally. Add egg and ¾ cup more flour or enough flour to make a thick batter. Beat at high speed two minutes, scraping bowl occasionally. Stir in enough additional flour to make a stiff batter. Cover bowl tightly with plastic wrap and refrigerate at least 2 hours or overnight. When ready to shape dough, combine the ½ cup flour, brown sugar, nuts and salt. Turn dough out onto a lightly floured board and divide in half. Roll half the dough into a 14 x 7-inch rectangle. Spread with ¾ cup cherries. Sprinkle with half the brown sugar mixture. Roll up from long side as for a jelly roll and seal edges. Place sealed edge down in a circle on a greased baking sheet. Pinch ends together. Cut slits 2/3 through the ring at 1-inch intervals. Twist each sliced section on its side. Make a second ring with remaining dough and filling. Cover and let rise in warm place until doubled, about 1 hour. Bake in a 375° oven about 20 to 25 minutes or until firm and browned. Remove from baking sheets and cool on wire racks. Frost with Confectioners' Sugar Frosting. Makes 2 coffee cakes.

CONFECTIONERS' SUGAR FROSTING

2 c. confectioners' sugar
2 T. (about) hot water or milk
1 t. vanilla or almond extract

Gradually stir hot water or milk into confectioners' sugar until the frosting is of a good spreading consistency. Add vanilla or almond extract.

Note: For a glaze, add more liquid.

CHEESE-FILLED SOUR CREAM COFFEE CAKE

1 8-oz. pkg. cream cheese, softened
2 egg yolks
½ c. sugar
½ t. vanilla
⅓ c. currants
2 t. lemon peel
¼ c. crushed cinnamon graham cracker crumbs
½ c. chopped walnuts
2 T. melted butter
½ c. butter
1 c. sugar
1 egg
2 egg whites
1 t. vanilla
2 c. flour
1 t. baking powder
1 t. baking soda
½ t. salt
1 c. sour cream

In a small mixing bowl, beat cream cheese, egg yolks, sugar and vanilla until blended. Stir in currants and lemon peel and set aside. In a small bowl mix crumbs and nuts. Stir in melted butter until well mixed; set aside. Cream butter with sugar until light and fluffy. Beat in egg and egg whites; add vanilla. Sift together flour, baking powder, soda and salt. Add to creamed mixture alternately with sour cream. Spread half of batter in a buttered 9-inch square pan. Spread cream cheese filling on top. Spoon remaining batter over, spreading carefully to cover filling. Sprinkle crumb mixture over batter. Bake in a 350° oven 50 to 55 minutes or until center springs back when touched lightly with finger. Cool 30 minutes before cutting. Makes 9 to 12 servings.

PLUM KUCHEN

½ c. butter or margarine
1 c. sugar
1 egg
½ c. sour cream
¼ t. vanilla
1 c. flour
½ t. baking powder
¼ t. salt
1 lb. fresh plums (about 6)
Cinnamon-sugar

In mixing bowl, cream butter with sugar. Add egg and beat until fluffy. Stir in sour cream and vanilla. Sift together flour, baking powder and salt. Fold into batter just until moistened. Spread batter in a greased and floured 9-inch layer cake pan. Quarter and pit plums. Arrange attractively on batter. Sprinkle cinnamon-sugar over plums. Bake in a 350° oven 50 to 60 minutes. Cool slightly and cut into wedges. Serve with sweetened whipped cream, if desired. Makes 8 servings.

COCONUT COFFEE CAKE

½ c. light brown sugar, firmly packed
2 T. flour
2 t. cinnamon
2 T. melted butter or margarine
⅔ c. flaked coconut
¾ c. sugar
¼ c. shortening
1 egg
½ c. milk
1½ c. flour
2 t. baking powder
½ t. salt

Combine brown sugar, flour, cinnamon, melted butter and coconut. Set aside. Cream sugar with the shortening; beat in egg. Add milk; stir in remaining ingredients. Spread half the batter in a greased and floured 8-inch square pan. Sprinkle with half of the coconut mixture. Add remaining batter, then rest of coconut mixture. Bake in a 375° oven for about 30 minutes. Makes 1 coffee cake.

MARY'S CINNAMON COFFEE CAKE

3 c. flour
1 c. brown sugar, firmly packed
1 c. sugar
1 T. cinnamon
1 c. butter, softened
1 t. salt
1 t. baking soda
1 t. vanilla
2 eggs, beaten
1 c. buttermilk

Combine flour, sugars, butter and cinnamon in a large mixing bowl. Mix as for a pie crust. Reserve ¾ cup of this mixture for topping. To the remaining mixture add salt, baking soda, vanilla and beaten eggs. Add buttermilk and blend ingredients until smooth; do not overbeat. Pour into a greased and floured tube pan or springform. Lightly sprinkle reserved topping over the top. Bake in a 350° oven 45 or 50 minutes or until a wooden pick inserted in center comes out clean. Cool before removing from the pan. Makes 1 large coffee cake.

LEMON SPICE COFFEE CAKE

1½ c. flour
1½ t. baking powder
½ t. baking soda
½ t. salt
¼ t. nutmeg
¼ t. cinnamon
⅓ c. butter
¾ c. sugar
1 egg
½ c. buttermilk
½ c. seedless raisins
1 t. grated lemon rind
¼ c. chopped walnuts

Sift together first 6 ingredients and set aside. Cream butter with sugar until fluffy. Beat in egg. Add sifted dry ingredients alternately with buttermilk, mixing well. Fold in raisins, lemon rind and nuts. Spread half the batter in a greased 8-inch square baking pan. Sprinkle with half the Crumb Topping. Spread with remaining batter and sprinkle remaining topping over top. Bake in a 350° oven 40 to 45 minutes. Serve warm. Makes 9 servings.

Crumb Topping

½ c. brown sugar, firmly packed
2 T. flour
¼ t. nutmeg
¼ t. cinnamon
　Dash salt
2 T. butter, melted
¼ c. chopped walnuts
1 t. grated lemon rind

Combine all ingredients, mixing well.

APPLE CRUMB COFFEE CAKE

¼ c. warm water
1 pkg. dry yeast
½ c. butter or margarine, softened
½ c. sugar
½ t. salt
3 eggs
¼ c. milk
2⅓ c. flour
2 or 3 large apples, cored and sliced
　Crumb Topping

Measure warm water into small warm bowl. Sprinkle in yeast and stir until dissolved. In large electric mixer bowl, cream butter or margarine with sugar and salt. Add yeast mixture, eggs and milk; beat at medium speed until well blended. Gradually add flour, still beating at medium speed; beat until mixture is blended well. Spread batter in a well-greased 9 x 9 x 2-inch square pan. Arrange apple slices on top and sprinkle Crumb Topping over. Cover and let rise in a warm place until doubled in bulk, about 1 hour. Bake in a 375° oven about 35 to 40 minutes. Turn out of pan and cool on wire rack. Makes one 9-inch square cake.

Crumb Topping

⅔ c. sugar
½ c. flour
2 t. cinnamon
6 T. butter or margarine

Combine all ingredients and mix until crumbly. Sprinkle over apples.

Sweet or soft doughs are more easily handled when fingers are lightly greased or floured. Work quickly . . . do as much as you can on lightly floured cloth or board. The warmth of your hands may make the dough sticky, but too much flour will result in a dry, compact product.

FRESH PEACH KUCHEN

1¼ c. flour
¼ c. sugar
½ t. salt
1 t. baking powder
½ c. butter
1 egg
1 T. milk
5 large peaches, sliced ½ inch thick
　Butter Streusel

Combine flour, sugar, salt and baking powder in a large bowl; cut in butter. Combine egg and milk and add to flour mixture, blending well. Spread on bottom and sides of a greased 8 x 12 x 2-inch pan. Arrange sliced peaches in lengthwise rows over the dough. Cover with Butter Streusel. Bake in a 350° oven 30 to 40 minutes. Serve warm. Makes 1 kuchen.

Butter Streusel

¾ c. sugar
2 T. flour
⅛ t. nutmeg
⅛ t. cinnamon
2 T. butter

Blend together all ingredients and sprinkle over peaches.

Pictured Opposite:
Gingerbread, p. 33

corn bread and quick breads

CORN BREAD

- 1 c. flour
- 3½ t. baking powder
- 1 t. salt
- 1½ T. sugar
- 1 c. yellow cornmeal
- 2 eggs
- 1 c. milk
- ¼ c. melted butter

Sift dry ingredients together into a large mixing bowl. Make a small hole in the center of the mixture. Add eggs and milk. Stir only until dry ingredients are moistened. Add melted butter. Pour batter into a greased 8 x 8 x 2-inch baking pan. Bake in a 400° oven 30 minutes or until lightly browned. Makes one 8 x 8-inch corn bread.

CORN BREAD

- 1 c. flour
- ¾ t. baking soda
- 1 t. baking powder
- 1 t. salt
- 1 c. yellow cornmeal
- ¼ c. melted butter
- 2 T. brown sugar, firmly packed
- 2 eggs, well beaten
- 1½ c. buttermilk

Sift flour, baking soda, baking powder and salt. Mix with cornmeal and set aside. Combine butter, brown sugar and eggs; add buttermilk. Stir into dry ingredients, beating only until smooth. Pour into a greased 9 x 9 x 2-inch baking pan. Bake in a 425° oven 25 to 30 minutes. Makes 9 servings.

CORN PONES

- 1 c. cornmeal
- ½ c. flour
- 3 t. baking powder
- 1 T. sugar
- ¾ c. milk
- 1 T. salad oil
- 1 egg

Combine all ingredients; stir only until well blended. Fill a greased corn stick pan 2/3 full. Bake in a 400° oven 15 minutes. Makes 10 to 12 servings.

CORN BRUNCH BREAD

- 2 c. milk
- ¾ c. yellow cornmeal
- 1 t. salt
- 2 T. butter
- 2 T. minced green pepper
- 1 17-oz. can whole kernel corn, drained
- 1 c. shredded Cheddar cheese
- 4 eggs, separated

Scald milk in medium saucepan; stir in cornmeal, salt and butter. When butter is melted, reduce heat. Add green pepper, corn, cheese and egg yolks, stirring until cheese is melted. Remove from heat. Beat egg whites until stiff and fold into corn mixture. Pour into a well-greased 11 x 7 x 1½-inch baking pan. Bake in a 350° oven 45 minutes. Serve warm with melted butter or maple syrup. Makes 8 to 10 servings.

Ever wonder just what the term "quick" bread means? Quick breads are those leavened by baking powder or soda, rather than with yeast. Loaf breads, such as banana or date-nut, biscuits, muffins, pancakes and waffles are all quick breads.

All quick breads should be mixed as for muffins. In other words, do not beat batters. Thoroughly blend dry ingredients then add combined liquid ingredients.

QUICK WHOLE WHEAT BREAD

- 4 c. whole wheat flour
- 2 c. flour
- ¾ c. sugar
- 2 t. salt
- ¼ c. sesame seed
- 1 qt. buttermilk
- 4 t. baking soda

Stir together first five ingredients. Combine buttermilk and baking soda; stir into flour mixture. Turn into 2 greased 9 x 5 x 3-inch loaf pans. Place in a 375° oven. *Immediately turn heat* to 350° and bake 60 minutes or until a cake tester inserted into center comes out clean. Remove from pans and cool on racks. Makes 2 loaves.

QUICK GRAHAM BREAD

1 c. flour
1½ t. baking soda
1 t. salt
½ c. brown sugar, firmly packed
2 c. buttermilk
2 c. graham flour

Sift flour, baking soda, salt and sugar together. Add buttermilk and graham flour, mixing only enough to moisten the flour. Pour into a greased 9 x 5 x 3-inch loaf pan. Bake in a 350° oven 60 minutes. Makes 1 loaf.

GINGERBREAD

1½ c. flour
½ t. baking powder
½ t. baking soda
1 t. salt
1½ t. ginger
¾ t. cinnamon
⅓ c. salad oil
½ c. brown sugar, firmly packed
1 egg, well-beaten
½ c. molasses
½ c. boiling water

Sift together first six ingredients. Make a well and add first the oil, then brown sugar and, lastly egg. Mix molasses and boiling water and add to batter. Beat until smooth. Turn into a greased 8-inch square pan. Bake in a 350° oven 35 to 40 minutes. Makes 6 to 8 servings.

PORK 'N' BEAN BREAD

2 c. flour
1 T. baking powder
1 t. salt
2 eggs, beaten
¼ c. salad oil
¼ c. dark brown sugar, firmly packed
¼ c. chopped cooked bacon
2 T. dry mustard
1 T. dry minced onion
1 16-oz. can pork and beans

Measure flour into mixing bowl with baking powder and salt. In another bowl, combine eggs, oil, sugar, bacon, mustard and onion; stir in beans. Add all at once to flour, stirring just until flour is moistened. Pour into a greased 8½ x 4½-inch loaf pan. Bake in a 350° oven 50 to 55 minutes or until done. Cool 15 minutes before removing from pan. Makes 1 loaf.

ORANGE CRACKLING BREAD

½ lb. salt pork, cut in cubes
2 T. finely chopped onion
1½ c. yellow cornmeal
½ c. flour
3 t. baking powder
1½ t. salt
1 t. sugar
2 eggs
½ c. buttermilk
1 c. orange juice

In a 9-inch oven-proof skillet, cook salt pork over low heat until very crisp; remove and chop fine. Drain off all but 1 tablespoon fat; add onion and cook until tender. In large bowl, mix together cornmeal, flour, baking powder, salt and sugar. In small bowl beat eggs with buttermilk and orange juice. Add egg mixture all at once to dry ingredients and stir just until mixed; stir in salt pork and onion. Heat the skillet, pour in batter and bake in a 350° oven 30 to 35 minutes. Serve hot with butter. Makes 8 servings.

PEANUT BUTTER-BACON BREAD

½ lb. bacon, cooked and crumbled
2 c. flour
1 c. sugar
3 t. baking powder
½ t. salt
1 c. peanut butter
1 t. melted butter
1 c. milk
1 egg, slightly beaten
1 c. chopped peanuts

Sift together flour, sugar, baking powder and salt. Cut in peanut butter until mixture is the consistency of cornmeal. Combine butter, milk and egg. Pour into peanut butter mixture and mix thoroughly. Stir in crumbled bacon and chopped peanuts. Pour into a greased and floured 9 x 5 x 3-inch loaf pan. Let stand 20 minutes. Bake in a 325° oven 1 hour and 15 minutes, or until a wooden pick inserted in center comes out clean. Cool on rack. Makes 1 loaf.

Quick breads are improved by resting the dough for 15 minutes before placing in the oven to bake. This allows the bread to rise just a little, but not enough to keep the top from cracking during the baking period.

biscuits, muffins, scones and popovers

BISCUITS

2 c. flour
1 T. baking powder
1 t. salt
¼ c. shortening
½ to ¾ c. milk

Stir together dry ingredients. Cut in shortening until mixture resembles coarse crumbs. Blend in enough milk to make a soft dough. Turn onto lightly floured surface and knead gently 30 seconds. Roll out ½ inch thick and cut biscuits with a floured cutter. Place on ungreased baking sheet and bake in a 450° oven 10 to 12 minutes, or until lightly browned. Makes 12 biscuits.

Muffins should be rounded on top with a slightly pebbly surface. The inside texture should be moist, tender and light. The grain should have round, even cells and be free from tunnels. Muffin batter must be pampered—most failures are caused by overmixing.

MUSHROOM BISCUITS

½ lb. fresh mushrooms *or* 1 8-oz. can mushrooms
1 T. butter
¼ c. minced onion
¼ t. ground thyme
　　Dash ground white pepper
2 c. buttermilk baking mix
½ c. milk

Rinse, drain and coarsely chop mushrooms. In a medium skillet, melt butter. Add onion and mushrooms and sauté 5 minutes. Stir in thyme and white pepper. Cool slightly. Blend mushroom mixture into baking mix. Add milk and combine lightly. Drop by tablespoonfuls onto greased cookie sheets, 2 inches apart. Bake in a 450° oven 12 minutes, or until browned. Serve with chicken, meat or fish. Makes 15 biscuits.

THREE-FLAVOR BISCUITS

2 c. flour
1 T. baking powder
1 t. salt
¼ c. shortening
5 slices crisp bacon, drained and crumbled
½ c. shredded Cheddar cheese
¼ c. finely chopped scallions
½ to ¾ c. milk

Sift together flour, baking powder and salt. Cut in shortening until mixture resembles coarse crumbs. Add bacon, cheese and scallions. Blend in enough milk to make a soft dough. Turn onto a lightly floured surface and knead gently 30 seconds. Roll out ½ inch thick and cut with a lightly floured biscuit cutter. Place on ungreased baking sheet. Bake in a 450° oven 10 to 12 minutes or until lightly browned. Makes 12 biscuits.

BUTTERMILK BISCUITS

2 c. flour
2½ t. baking powder
½ t. baking soda
1 t. salt
⅓ c. plus 2 t. lard
¾ c. buttermilk
　　Melted butter

Sift together first 4 ingredients into a mixing bowl. Cut in lard with a fork or pastry blender. Stir in buttermilk. Mix only until all dry ingredients are moistened. Turn onto a lightly floured board, turning several times to form a round ball. Pat out into a circle, ½ to ¾ inch thick. Cut with a small floured glass or biscuit cutter and place on a greased baking sheet. Brush tops with melted butter. Bake in a 450° oven 12 to 15 minutes. Serve piping hot. Makes 14 to 16 biscuits.

A light and gentle touch both in mixing and handling the dough is the secret of good biscuits.

Pictured Opposite:
Corn Pones, p. 32

BLUEBERRY MUFFINS

2 c. flour
3 T. sugar
3 t. baking powder
½ t. salt
¼ t. mace
¾ c. milk
1 egg
3 T. melted butter or margarine
1 t. vanilla
1 c. fresh blueberries
1 T. butter or margarine
¼ c. sugar
1 t. cinnamon

Combine first five ingredients. Add milk, egg, butter and vanilla. Mix just until dry ingredients are moistened. Lightly fold in blueberries. Spoon into well-greased muffin pans. Combine butter, sugar and cinnamon. Sprinkle over top of muffin batter before baking. Bake in a 425° oven 20 to 25 minutes. Makes 10 to 12 muffins.

CINNAMON RAISIN ENGLISH MUFFINS

3½ to 4 c. flour
2 pkgs. dry yeast
2 T. cinnamon
1 c. milk
¼ c. water
½ c. seedless raisins
2 T. sugar
2 T. vegetable oil
1 t. salt
Cornmeal
Butter

Stir together 1½ cups flour, yeast and cinnamon. Heat milk, water, raisins, sugar, oil and salt over low heat until warm. Add liquid ingredients to flour-yeast mixture and beat until smooth, about 1 minute by hand. Stir in more flour to make a soft dough. Turn out onto lightly floured board and knead until manageable, about 3 minutes. Cover dough with bowl or pan and let rest 30 minutes. Sprinkle cornmeal on a flat surface; place dough on cornmeal and roll out ½ inch thick. Cut into circles with a 3 or 4-inch cutter. Sprinkle cornmeal on top and let muffins rest about 30 minutes or until lightly raised. Sprinkle cornmeal in a skillet and preheat it to medium-hot. Place muffins in and bake 15 to 18 minutes on each side. Reduce heat if necessary to avoid over-browning. When cool, split, toast and butter. Makes 10 to 12 muffins.

"BRER" RABBIT MUFFINS

2 c. flour
1 T. baking powder
½ t. cinnamon
1 t. salt
¼ t. ground cloves
¼ t. nutmeg
1 egg, beaten
¾ c. milk
3 T. salad oil
½ c. chunky peanut butter
¼ c. dark molasses
2 T. brown sugar
Chopped peanuts

Stir together first 6 ingredients. Combine egg, milk, oil, peanut butter, molasses and brown sugar. Add liquid all at once to flour mixture, stirring only until flour is moistened. Fill greased muffin cups two-thirds full. Sprinkle each muffin with chopped peanuts. Bake in a 425° oven 20 to 25 minutes, or until golden brown. Makes 12 muffins.

Do you know the difference between "dough" and "batter"? Any mixture thick enough to be rolled or kneaded is called a dough. A mixture that is thin enough to be poured or dropped from a spoon is known as a batter.

APRICOT OATMEAL MUFFINS

2 c. flour
½ c. rolled oats
½ c. sugar
1 T. baking powder
1 t. salt
2 t. pumpkin pie spice
1 c. chopped dried apricots
½ c. chopped nuts
2 eggs
1⅓ c. milk
¼ c. salad oil

Stir together flour, oats, sugar, baking powder, salt and spice. Add apricots and nuts; stir to blend. Beat together eggs, milk and oil. Add all at once to flour mixture, stirring only until all the flour is moistened. Fill greased muffin cups two-thirds full. Bake in a 350° oven 25 to 30 minutes or until golden brown. Makes 24 muffins.

SCONES

1¾ c. sifted flour
2¼ t. baking powder
2 T. sugar
½ t. salt
⅓ c. butter or margarine, softened
¾ c. currants
2 eggs, beaten
⅓ c. heavy cream

Sift together flour, baking powder, sugar and salt. Cut in butter until particles are the size of small peas. Fold in currants. Reserve 2 tablespoons egg for brushing tops. Combine remaining egg and cream; add to dry ingredients. Stir just until all flour is moistened. Place on a lightly floured board; pat to ½ inch thick. Cut into diamond shapes; brush with reserved egg and sprinkle with salt or sugar, if desired. Place on an ungreased baking sheet. Bake in a 450° oven 12 to 15 minutes. Makes 12 to 15 scones.

WALNUT WHOLE WHEAT SCONES

1½ c. flour
3 T. sugar
3 t. baking powder
¾ t. salt
½ c. whole wheat flour
½ c. butter
2 eggs
⅓ c. milk
½ c. walnuts, coarsely chopped

Sift flour with sugar, baking powder and salt. Stir in whole wheat flour. Cut in butter until particles resemble coarse meal. Beat eggs. Reserve 1 tablespoon egg to brush top of scones. Combine remainder of eggs with milk and stir into dry mixture. Reserve 2 tablespoons walnuts, stir in remainder. Turn out onto a greased baking sheet. With floured hands, pat out dough to an 8-inch circle. Cut two-thirds through into 8 wedges. Brush tops with reserved egg and sprinkle with remaining walnuts. Bake in a 400° oven 20 minutes, or until nicely browned. Cut scones apart and serve hot. Makes 8 scones.

Lumpy—that's the batter for perfect muffins. Overbeaten batter will cause peaks, tunnels and toughness in the muffins because the gluten in the flour is over-developed.

MELLOW MUFFINS

1 c. seedless raisins
2 c. sifted flour
⅓ c. brown sugar, firmly packed
3 t. baking powder
1 t. cinnamon
½ t. salt
¼ t. baking soda
1 egg
⅔ c. milk
½ c. (1 medium) mashed ripe banana
¼ c. melted margarine or butter

Combine first 7 ingredients; set aside. Combine egg, milk, banana and margarine; mix well and add to dry ingredients. Stir until all flour is moistened. Fill greased muffin pans two-thirds full. Bake in a 400° oven 20 to 25 minutes. Serve immediately. Makes 12 medium muffins.

Scones are popular fare throughout the British Isles. The English rhyme "scone" with "gone." All good Scots get a gleam in their eye when they talk about their traditional quick bread. Even the Irish serve the delicious wedge-shaped scone for breakfast or tea with plenty of butter and orange marmalade.

CURRANT SCONES

2 c. flour
1 T. baking powder
1 t. salt
⅓ c. shortening
2 eggs
½ c. milk
2 T. honey or corn syrup
¼ c. currants

Stir together flour, baking powder and salt. Cut in shortening. Beat 1 whole egg and 1 egg yolk, reserving the other egg white. Add milk, 1 tablespoon of the honey or corn syrup and currants to beaten egg; add all at once to flour mixture. Stir only enough to moisten flour. Turn onto a lightly floured surface and knead gently for 30 seconds. Place on an ungreased baking sheet; roll out to a 9-inch square. Cut into 9 squares. Beat egg white until frothy; add remaining honey or corn syrup and brush over top of dough. Bake in a 425° oven 12 to 15 minutes or until golden brown. Makes 9 scones.

Yankee settlers made their own version of English Yorkshire Pudding. They called it "popovers." Using heavy cast-iron pans resembling muffin pans but with straighter sides, they baked a thin batter that "popped over the sides." Some folks called these pop-puffs. The big, puffy steam-raised quick bread was one of the alternative breads homemakers made before the advent of reliable baking powder.

Popovers are the first cousins of cream puffs; they contain the same ingredients. Popover batter is thin whereas cream puff batter is very stiff. In each, steam formed during the first few minutes of baking is the leavening agent.

POPOVERS

1 c. flour
¼ t. salt
1 T. sugar
1 c. milk
2 eggs, slightly beaten
1 T. melted butter

Mix flour, salt and sugar in a bowl; add milk, eggs and butter. Beat with rotary beaters until very smooth. Do not overbeat as this will decrease volume. Fill well-greased large muffin cups half full. Bake in a 375° oven about 50 minutes or until brown and firm to the touch. Remove from cups and serve hot with butter. Makes about 9 popovers.

ONION POPOVERS

3 eggs, well beaten
1 c. milk
2 T. dry onion soup mix
1 T. salad oil
1 c. flour

Combine eggs, milk, onion soup mix and oil. Blend in flour until smooth. Beat 1 minute with electric mixer or 3 minutes with rotary beater. Fill well-greased popover pans or custard cups half full. Bake in lower part of a 425° oven 40 to 45 minutes until brown and firm to touch. For crisper popovers, prick sides to release steam. Reduce oven temperature to 350° and bake 20 minutes longer. Makes 6 large or 11 small popovers.

CHOCOLATE CHIP MUFFINS

2 c. flour
1 T. baking powder
1 t. salt
1 c. milk
3 T. melted butter
1 egg, beaten
1 t. vanilla
½ c. light brown sugar, firmly packed
1 6-oz. pkg. semisweet chocolate chips

Stir together flour, baking powder and salt. In a separate bowl, combine milk, butter, egg, vanilla, brown sugar and chocolate chips. Add chocolate chip mixture to flour mixture, stirring only until flour is moistened. Batter should be lumpy. Fill 12 greased muffin cups two-thirds full. Bake in a 425° oven 20 to 25 minutes or until muffins are golden brown. Makes 12 muffins.

So you think "bringing home the bread," or dough, is a modern expression? Not so. For hundreds of years, wages were paid in bread. The average Egyptian peasant earned three loaves and two jugs of beer a day.

APRICOT WALNUT MUFFINS

1½ c. flour
2 t. baking powder
½ t. salt
½ t. cinnamon
½ c. sugar
½ c. finely chopped dried apricots
½ c. finely chopped walnuts
1 egg, slightly beaten
1 c. milk
¼ c. salad oil

Sift together flour, baking powder, salt, cinnamon and sugar. Stir in apricots and walnuts. Combine remaining ingredients and add to dry mixture. Stir just until ingredients are mixed. Spoon into 12 greased 2¾-inch muffin cups or 42 greased 1½-inch muffin cups. (Fill each muffin cup two-thirds full.) Bake in a 425° oven until a wooden pick inserted in center comes out clean, about 25 minutes for 2¾-inch muffins and 12 to 15 minutes for 1½-inch muffins. Serve warm with butter. (Makes 1 dozen large muffins or 3½ dozen small muffins.)

Pictured Opposite:
Apricot Walnut Muffins

ethnic breads

ANISE LOAF

1 pkg. dry yeast
¼ c. warm water
½ c. milk, scalded
⅓ c. sugar
¼ c. butter
½ t. salt
¼ t. oil of anise
6 drops oil of cinnamon
2¾ to 3 c. flour
1 egg
1 egg in shell, uncooked, tinted red
1 egg, slightly beaten
1 T. water
2 T. sesame seed

Soften dry yeast in warm water and set aside. Pour scalded milk over sugar, butter and salt, stirring until butter melts. Cool to lukewarm. Stir in flavorings. Add 1 cup of the flour; mix well. Stir in 1 egg and softened yeast; beat well. Add remaining flour or enough to make a soft dough. Turn out on a lightly floured surface. Cover and let rest 10 minutes. Knead until smooth and elastic. Place in a lightly greased bowl, turning once to grease surface. Cover; let rise in warm place until doubled in bulk. Punch down; let rise again until almost doubled. Turn out on a lightly floured surface and divide dough in thirds. Form in balls. Cover and let rest 10 minutes. Using your hands, roll each part to form a strand, 16-inches long, tapering ends. Line up strands 1 inch apart on a greased baking sheet. Braid loosely without stretching dough, beginning in middle and working toward either end. Pinch ends together. Tuck tinted uncooked egg, large end up, in center of braid. Cover and let rise until almost doubled, about 40 minutes. Combine beaten egg and water; brush over braid; sprinkle with sesame seed. Bake in a 375° oven about 25 minutes or until golden. Makes 1 loaf.

Does your bread smell and taste yeasty? This is an indication that the bread has risen too long. It does not indicate the presence of too much yeast.

IRISH FRECKLE BREAD

1¼ c. dehydrated or frozen hashed brown potatoes
2 cakes yeast
½ c. warm water
2 eggs, slightly beaten
½ c. sugar
2 t. salt
½ t. ground mace
1 c. dried currants or raisins
½ c. melted butter
5½ c. sifted flour

Reconstitute potatoes as directed on package and drain well (or let frozen potatoes thaw). Set aside 1 tablespoon beaten egg. Soften yeast in warm water; mix with eggs, potatoes, sugar, salt, mace, currants and melted butter. Add enough flour to make a fairly stiff dough. Knead several minutes. Let rise in a warm place until doubled in bulk. Punch dough down and shape into one large round loaf or two small ones and place on a greased cookie sheet. Brush with reserved egg and put immediately into a 375° oven. Bake 50 to 60 minutes until nicely browned. Best served warm; bread can be reheated if necessary. Makes 12 servings.

NEAR-EASTERN WHEAT BREAD

2 c. whole wheat flour
2 to 2½ c. flour
2 pkgs. dry yeast
1 t. salt
1½ c. lukewarm water

Combine whole wheat flour, 1 cup flour and yeast. Dissolve salt in lukewarm water and add to flour mixture, mixing well. Stir in more flour to make a moderately stiff dough. Turn onto a lightly floured surface and knead 20 minutes. Shape into a ball and place in a lightly greased bowl, turning to grease all sides. Cover and let rise in a warm place until doubled in bulk, about 1½ hours. Divide dough into 3 equal parts; roll each ½ inch thick. Place on an ungreased baking sheet and bake in a 350° oven 40 to 45 minutes or until done. Makes 3 loaves.

DANISH KRINGLE

1 cake compressed yeast
½ c. lukewarm water
4 c. flour
1 t. salt
3 T. sugar
1 c. lard
3 eggs, separated
1 c. milk
¾ c. brown sugar
½ c. chopped nuts, raisins, or
    cooked fruit

Dissolve yeast in lukewarm water. Sift flour, salt and sugar together in a large mixing bowl. Blend in lard as for a pie crust. Beat egg yolks; add milk and beat again. Add egg and milk mixture and yeast to flour mixture. Cover and store in refrigerator overnight. Divide dough into 3 or 4 parts, depending on size of cookie sheets. Roll each piece of dough to about ¼ inch thick, about 9 inches wide and the length of the pan. Place dough on baking sheet; spread with stiffly beaten egg whites. Mix sugar with nuts and fruit. Spread over egg whites through the center third of the dough. Fold one-third of the dough about halfway over filling; fold remaining one-third over the top. Let rise 2 hours. Bake in a 350° oven about 30 minutes, or until done and lightly browned. Ice with confectioners' sugar frosting while still hot. Kringle will bake to about 1 inch or less thickness. Makes 3 or 4 Kringles.

FINNISH COUNTRY BREAD

2 c. hot water
2 T. sugar
2 T. butter
2 t. salt
5½ to 6 c. flour
1 pkg. dry yeast

Combine hot water, sugar, butter and salt in a large mixing bowl; mix at low speed of electric mixer until butter melts. Blend in 2 cups flour with yeast and beat until smooth, about 2 minutes on medium speed. Blend in 2 more cups flour; beat well, about 2 to 3 minutes on medium speed. Stir in more flour to make a moderately stiff dough. Turn onto a lightly floured surface and knead until smooth and satiny, 8 to 10 minutes. Shape into a ball and place in a lightly greased bowl, turning to grease all sides. Cover and let rise in warm place until doubled in bulk, about 1½ hours. Punch down and knead lightly for 1 minute, then divide in half. Shape each half into a ball; let rest 10 minutes. Place on a greased baking sheet and roll out to a circle, ½ inch thick. Cover and let rise until nearly doubled in bulk, about ½ hour. Prick with a fork and bake in a 400° oven 20 to 25 minutes or until golden brown. Makes 2 loaves.

ITALIAN PANETTONE

2 pkgs. dry yeast
½ c. sugar
2 t. salt
6 to 6½ c. flour
1 c. water
½ c. butter or margarine
1 t. grated lemon peel
4 eggs
1½ c. raisins (mixed golden and regular)
⅓ c. pine nuts (reserve 1 T. for garnish)
1 c. mixed, chopped candied fruits
    Melted butter
    Confectioners' sugar

In a large mixer bowl, combine yeast, sugar salt and 2 cups of the flour. Heat water with butter and lemon peel over low heat until very warm (120 to 130°). Add liquid to dry ingredients; beat for 2 minutes at medium speed. Add 2 cups more of the flour and the eggs; beat 3 minutes. Stir in almost all of the remaining flour. Knead dough on floured board about 8 minutes until smooth and elastic. Place in a buttered bowl, cover and let rise in warm place until doubled in bulk, about 2 hours. Punch down; knead in raisins, nuts and fruit. Shape into 2 round loaves and place in 2 greased 9-inch cake pans; brush lightly with melted butter. Let rise 1 to 1½ hours until doubled in bulk. With a sharp knife, slash the top of each loaf to make a cross. Bake in a 350° oven 45 to 55 minutes. Turn onto rack. Brush lightly with butter. Garnish with remaining pine nuts. Dust with confectioners' sugar. Serve with Orange Butter. Makes 2 loaves.

ORANGE BUTTER

½ c. butter or margarine
1½ c. confectioners' sugar
2 T. orange juice
1 T. grated orange peel
    Dash angostura bitters

Combine all ingredients and beat until fluffy. Serve as a spread for Panettone. Makes 1 cup.

KUGELHOPF

½ c. raisins
¼ c. rum
¾ c. milk
1 13¾-oz. pkg. hot roll mix
2 eggs, slightly beaten
4 T. melted butter or margarine
¼ c. sugar
1 t. grated lemon peel
½ t. ground mace
½ c. chopped walnuts
1 T. melted butter or margarine
3 T. fine dry bread crumbs

Soak raisins in rum; let stand until plump. Drain and set aside. Heat milk to warm (115° to 120°); add yeast from hot roll mix and stir to dissolve. Combine eggs, 4 tablespoons melted butter, sugar, lemon peel, mace and yeast mixture. Add flour from mix; beat smooth by hand. Stir in raisins and walnuts. Cover and let rise in warm place until doubled in bulk, about 1½ to 2 hours. Meanwhile, brush a 2-quart fluted tube pan or kugelhopf mold with the 1 tablespoon melted butter and sprinkle with dry bread crumbs. Stir down batter and spoon carefully into mold. Let rise until almost doubled in bulk, about 50 to 60 minutes. Bake in a 350° oven for 25 to 30 minutes; cool in pan 10 minutes. Remove from pan and cool on rack. Makes 1 coffee cake.

FRENCH CROISSANTS

¾ c. margarine
¼ c. flour
2½ to 3 c. flour
3 T. sugar
1 t. salt
1 pkg. dry yeast
¾ c. milk
¼ c. water
2 eggs (at room temperature)
1 T. milk
Sugar

Cut margarine into ¼ cup flour until mixture is a smooth paste. Place between two sheets of waxed paper and roll into a 10 x 4-inch rectangle. Chill 1 hour. When mixture is chilled, prepare dough by mixing 1 cup flour, sugar, salt and dry yeast. Set aside. Combine ¾ cup milk and water in a saucepan. Heat over low heat until very warm (120° to 130°). Gradually add to dry ingredients and beat 2 minutes at medium speed of electric mixer, scraping bowl occasionally. Add 1 egg and ½ cup flour; beat at high speed 2 minutes, scraping bowl occasionally. Stir in enough additional flour to make a soft dough. Turn out onto a heavily floured board and roll out to a 12-inch square. Carefully peel waxed paper from chilled margarine mixture; place over center third of dough. Fold outside third of dough over margarine slab; cover with remaining third of dough. Turn dough over a quarter turn, then roll out to a 12-inch square. Fold as above. Turn dough, roll and fold 3 more times. Wrap in waxed paper and chill 2 hours or overnight. Proceed according to directions below for desired variations.

BREAKFAST-SIZE CROISSANTS

Divide dough into 3 equal pieces and shape one piece at a time, refrigerating the remainder. On a floured board, roll out 1 piece into a 10-inch circle. Cut circle into quarters. Beat 1 egg with 1 tablespoon milk; brush point of each piece with egg mixture. Roll up each piece tightly, beginning at wide end; seal points. Place on greased baking sheets, turning points under. Curve to form crescents; brush with egg mixture and sprinkle with sugar. Repeat with remaining dough, egg mixture and sugar. Let rise, uncovered, in a warm place about 30 minutes until light. Bake in a 375° oven 15 to 18 minutes or until done. Remove from baking sheets and cool on wire racks. Best when served warm. Makes 12.

MINIATURE CROISSANTS

Proceed as for Breakfast-Size Croissants except divide the dough into 6 equal pieces. Roll each piece into an 8-inch circle and cut into 8 wedge-shaped pieces. Bake in a 375° oven 12 minutes or until done. Makes 48.

CHEESE TWISTS

Blend ½ cup grated Parmesan cheese to margarine and flour. Prepare dough as for Breakfast-Size Croissants only divide dough into 4 equal pieces. Roll each piece into an 8 x 6-inch rectangle; cut into eight 1-inch strips. Twist each strip to form a 6-inch spiral; place on greased baking sheets. Beat together 1 egg with 1 tablespoon milk. Brush twists with egg mixture. Let rise, uncovered, in a warm place about 30 minutes until light. Bake in a 375° oven about 12 minutes or until done. Makes 12.

Pictured Opposite:
Popovers, p. 39

SWEDISH RYE BREAD

    1 pkg. dry yeast
    1 c. lukewarm water
    1 c. milk, scalded
    ⅓ c. butter or margarine
    2 T. sugar
    1½ t. salt
    ¾ c. dark corn syrup
    3 c. rye flour
    4½ c. (about) sifted flour
    1 t. fennel seed
    1 t. anise seed
    1 t. grated orange rind
      Lukewarm water

Dissolve yeast in lukewarm water. In a large bowl, mix together scalded milk, butter, sugar, salt and corn syrup. Cool to lukewarm. Add yeast to milk mixture; stir in rye flour and enough flour to form a soft, but not sticky, dough. Add fennel, anise seed and orange rind. Knead dough on a lightly floured surface until smooth, about 10 minutes. Form into a ball and place in a greased bowl. Grease top of dough with corn oil. Cover and let rise in a warm place until doubled in bulk, 1 to 1½ hours. Punch down dough. Knead about 1 minute. Divide in half. Shape into loaves. Place in 2 greased 9 x 5 x 3-inch loaf pans. Cover and let rise until doubled in bulk, about 45 minutes. Bake in a 375° oven 45 minutes. Brush tops with lukewarm water. Bake 5 minutes longer. Turn out onto a wire rack to cool. Makes 2 loaves.

BRIOCHE

    4½ c. flour (about)
    1 pkg. dry yeast
    ½ c. milk
    ¼ c. water
    ½ c. butter
    ¼ c. sugar
    1 t. salt
    2 eggs
      Melted butter

Stir together 1 cup flour and yeast. Heat milk, water, butter, sugar and salt over low heat only until warm, stirring to blend. Add liquid ingredients to flour-yeast mixture and beat until smooth, about 2 minutes on medium speed of electric mixer or 300 strokes by hand. Cover and let rise in a warm place until bubbly, about 1 hour. Stir down and beat in eggs. Add more flour to make a soft dough. Turn onto a lightly floured surface and knead until smooth and satiny, about 20 minutes. Shape into a ball and place in a lightly greased bowl, turning to grease all sides. Cover and let rise in a warm place until doubled in bulk, about 1½ hours. Punch dough down and let rest 10 minutes. Remove about one-fifth of the dough; shape each portion into a smooth ball. Place large ball in a greased 1¾-quart brioche or baking mold. Make an indentation in the center of the large ball; place a smaller ball in the indentation. Let rise in warm place until doubled in bulk, about 40 minutes. Bake in a 350° oven 40 to 45 minutes or until golden brown and firm. Immediately remove from mold and brush top with butter. Serve warm or cool. Makes 10 to 12 servings.

ITALIAN EASTER BREAD

    2 pkgs. dry yeast
    ½ c. warm water
    1 c. milk, scalded
    ½ c. sugar
    1 t. salt
    1 t. ground anise
    4 egg yolks
    1 T. grated orange or lemon peel
    2 T. lemon juice
    6 c. flour (about)
    ½ c. melted butter or margarine
    6 hard-boiled eggs, lightly tinted

Soften yeast in warm water. Mix sugar with salt and anise and add to lukewarm milk. Beat egg yolks and blend with yeast mixture. Stir in orange or lemon peel, lemon juice and 1½ cups of the flour. Beat batter until it falls in sheets from spoon, beat in melted butter. Stir in remaining flour and turn out onto a lightly floured board and knead until smooth and satiny. Place dough in a large greased bowl. Turn dough to grease on all sides. Cover bowl and let rise in a warm place (80° to 85°) until doubled in bulk, about 1 hour. Divide dough into 2 parts. Shape into 2 balls, cover and let rest 10 minutes. Roll each ball in a long roll about 30 inches long and 1 to 1½ inches thick. Twist the 2 pieces together loosely. Shape into a ring. Place on a lightly greased 15½ x 12-inch baking sheet. Make 6 holes in the top of the dough. Place a lightly tinted hard-boiled egg in each. Cover and let rise in a warm place until doubled in bulk. Remove egg and bake in a 350° oven 35 minutes or until bread is golden brown. Place eggs back in bread centers when serving. Makes one 15-inch ring.

GERMAN SOUR CREAM TWISTS

3½ c. flour
1 t. salt
1 c. butter
1 pkg. dry yeast *or* 1 cake compressed
    yeast
1 c. sour cream
1 egg
2 egg yolks
1 t. vanilla
1 c. sugar

Sift flour and salt together into a large bowl. Cut in butter, leaving lumps the size of large peas. Combine yeast, sour cream, egg and egg yolks, beating well. Add vanilla. Add to flour-yeast mixture. Mix thoroughly, using hands if necessary. Dough will be stiff. Cover dough with damp cloth. Chill in refrigerator at least 2 hours or overnight; dough should be very cold and firm. Remove one-half of dough from refrigerator. Generously sprinkle board with sugar. Turn dough out onto sugared surface. Roll out into an 8 x 16-inch rectangle. Fold two ends into center, allowing one end to overlap the other. Sprinkle with sugar and roll out to same size again. Repeat two times. Roll dough out to ¼-inch thickness. Cut into strips 1 inch wide by 4 inches long. Twist ends of each strip in opposite directions, stretching dough gently and slightly. Place twists in the form of horseshoes on ungreased baking sheet and pressing down ends to keep twists in shape. Repeat process with second half of dough. Bake at once in a 375° oven for 15 minutes or until delicately brown. Remove immediately from baking sheet. Makes about 4 dozen Twists.

A charming Hungarian legend claims lovely Queen Elizabeth secretly carried bread to the poor each day under her mantle. Once she met her mean husband returning from a chase. He demanded she open the folds of the mantle. Imagine their surprise as the rolls in the basket she carried turned into red and white roses.

ROSCA DE REYES
(Mexican Three Kings Coffee Cake)

2 pkgs. dry yeast
¼ c. lukewarm water
1 c. milk
6½ c. sifted flour
1 c. butter or margarine
2 t. ground cinnamon
½ c. sugar
3 eggs
1 t. salt
1 T. grated orange rind
1 T. grated lemon rind
½ c. coarsely chopped nuts
½ c. seedless raisins
2 T. chopped glacé cherries
    Confectioners' sugar and
    Water Frosting
    Glacé cherries and toasted blanched
    almonds
½ 1-oz. square chocolate, melted

Soften yeast in lukewarm water for 5 minutes. Scald milk; cool to lukewarm. Add milk to softened yeast along with 1 cup of the sifted flour and beat well. Cover and let stand 30 minutes. Cream butter or margarine until soft and fluffy. Gradually add cinnamon and sugar. Beat in eggs, one at a time; add yeast mixture and beat again. Stir in salt and remaining flour to make a soft, easily handled dough. Knead on a lightly floured board until smooth and elastic and place in a greased bowl. Turn once to coat with grease. Cover and let rise, 1½ hours or until doubled in bulk. On a lightly floured board, knead in orange and lemon rinds, nuts, raisins and cherries. Divide dough in half and form each half into a long, narrow roll. Join the ends of each roll to form a circle and place on a greased baking sheet. Cover and let rise until doubled in bulk. With a very sharp knife, make tiny slashes in the top of the crown about 2 inches apart. Bake in a 400° oven 20 minutes. Cool. Frost with Confectioners' Sugar and Water Frosting. Garnish with glacé cherries and whole almonds dipped in chocolate. Makes 2 coffee cakes.

CONFECTIONERS' SUGAR AND WATER FROSTING

Stir about 4 teaspoons water into 1 cup confectioners' sugar. Makes enough for two coffee rings, 12 to 13 inches diameter.

SCOTTISH SCONES

1¼ c. sifted flour
⅓ c. sugar
2 t. baking powder
½ t. salt
¼ c. shortening
¼ c. butter or margarine
1 c. quick or old-fashioned oats
¼ c. currants or raisins
⅓ c. milk
1 T. sugar
⅛ t. cinnamon
   Melted butter

Sift together flour, sugar, baking powder and salt. Cut in shortening and butter until mixture resembles coarse crumbs; mix in oats and currants. Add milk, mixing just until dry ingredients are moistened. Turn dough out on a lightly floured surface; knead gently 5 times. Roll to form a 6 to 7-inch circle. Combine remaining sugar with cinnamon. Brush top of dough with melted butter and sprinkle lightly with cinnamon-sugar. Cut into 6 pie-shaped wedges. Place on an ungreased cookie sheet and bake in a 375° oven about 15 minutes. Serve warm with orange marmalade, if desired. Makes 6 scones.

GERMAN PLUM DUMPLINGS

2½ c. water
1 7-oz. pkg. instant mashed potatoes
4 eggs
2 c. flour
1 t. salt
¼ t. nutmeg
12 blue prune plums
12 sugar cubes
   Boiling salted water
½ c. butter or margarine
3 c. soft bread crumbs

Heat water to boiling. Beat in potatoes; mixture will be very dry and crumbly. Beat in eggs, flour, salt and nutmeg. Knead on a heavily floured board until smooth and firm to the touch. Cut dough into 12 pieces. Flatten dough out into 3-inch rounds. Pit plums and replace pit with a sugar cube. Wrap dough around plums, sealing edges well. Drop dumplings into boiling water and cook for 10 minutes. Drain and place on a serving dish. Heat butter and sauté crumbs until golden brown. Sprinkle crumbs over dumplings. Serve hot. Makes 12 dumplings.

Pictured Opposite:
Scones, p. 37

BIRNBROT
(Swiss Pear Bread)

½ c. milk
1 pkg. dry yeast
1 t. plus ¼ c. sugar, divided
2½ c. flour, divided
¼ c. shortening
1 egg
⅛ t. salt
   Fruit Filling

Scald milk; cool to lukewarm. Pour into a deep mixing bowl. Sprinkle yeast and 1 teaspoon of the sugar over milk; let stand 3 minutes then blend. Place in a warm place for 5 minutes or until yeast bubbles. Gradually beat in ½ cup of the flour, stirring constantly. Beat in shortening; add egg, remaining ¼ cup sugar and salt. Beat in remaining flour, ½ cup at a time and blend to form a dough. Knead on a lightly floured board until smooth and elastic. Shape dough into a ball and place in a well-greased bowl. Cover and set in a warm place until dough doubles in bulk, about 1 hour. Punch down dough; turn onto a lightly floured board and roll into a 16-inch square, ¼ inch thick. Spread Fruit Filling over dough to within 1 inch of edges. Fold edges over the filling to make a 14-inch square, then roll dough jelly-roll fashion. Place on a buttered baking sheet; prick top surface with a fork. Let rise 1 hour. Brush with egg wash, if desired. Bake in a 350° oven 30 to 35 minutes. Serve warm, if desired. Makes 1 loaf.

Fruit Filling

1⅔ c. water
1 8-oz. pkg. dried pears, chopped
½ c. chopped pitted prunes
½ c. seedless raisins
2 T. lemon juice
½ c. finely chopped walnuts
⅓ c. sugar
2 T. vanilla
1 T. grated lemon peel
1 t. ground cinnamon
½ t. ground nutmeg
¼ t. ground allspice

In a small saucepan, bring water to a boil. Add pears, prunes, raisins and lemon juice. Reduce heat and simmer, stirring frequently, until fruit is tender. Put in blender jar and puree. Turn into bowl. Add nuts, sugar, vanilla, lemon peel, cinnamon, nutmeg and allspice; blend well. Makes enough for 1 loaf.

SWEDISH LIMPA BREAD

2 pkgs. dry yeast
⅓ c. sugar
1 T. salt
2½ c. flour
1½ c. water
¼ c. molasses
2 T. shortening
1 T. fennel seed, finely crushed
2 T. anise seed, finely crushed
2 T. grated orange rind
2½ c. rye flour
1½ c. raisins
Melted butter

In a large mixing bowl, combine yeast, sugar, salt and 2 cups of the flour. Heat water with molasses and shortening over low heat until very warm (120 to 130°). Add liquids to dry ingredients in bowl. Beat for 2 minutes at medium speed. Add fennel and anise seed, orange rind and 2 cups of the rye flour; beat 3 minutes. Knead dough on floured board, using remaining flours, until smooth and elastic. Cover and let rise in a warm place about 1½ hours or until doubled in bulk. Punch down; knead in raisins. Shape into 2 oval leaves; place on greased baking sheet and let rise about 1 hour until doubled in bulk. Bake in 375° oven 30 to 35 minutes. Brush tops of warm loaves with melted butter. Cool on racks. Slice when cold. Makes 2 loaves.

The Scandinavians invited God's blessing on their breads by making the sign of the cross over the grain, over the dough, in front of the oven and over the baked bread.

IRISH SODA BREAD

2 c. flour
1 T. sugar
1½ t. baking powder
1 t. baking soda
¼ t. salt
¼ c. butter or margarine, softened
¾ c. raisins
1½ t. caraway seed (optional)
1 c. buttermilk
1 egg, slightly beaten with 1 T. water

Sift flour, sugar, baking powder, soda and salt into a large mixing bowl. Cut in butter with a pastry blender until mixture resembles coarse meal. Stir in raisins and caraway seed. Add buttermilk, blending to moisten the dry ingredients. Turn dough onto a floured board; knead for several

minutes until smooth. Form dough into a round ball and place on a greased baking sheet. Flatten ball until dough is about 1½ inches high; brush top and sides with egg-water mixture. Cut a ½-inch deep cross in top of bread with sharp knife. Bake in a 375° oven 30 to 40 minutes or until a wooden pick inserted in center comes out clean. Transfer to wire rack to cool; brush top with butter or margarine and cover with cloth. Makes 1 round loaf.

FRENCH BREAD

2 pkgs. dry yeast
½ c. warm water (110 to 115°)
1 t. sugar
1 T. salt
2 T. butter
2 c. lukewarm water (90°)
7 to 7½ c. flour
1 egg, slightly beaten with 1 T. water

Soften yeast in warm water. Let stand 5 minutes. Add sugar, salt, butter, lukewarm water and half of the flour; beat well. Work in remaining flour. Turn dough onto a lightly floured board and shape into a ball. Cover with bowl and let rest 10 minutes. Knead 10 minutes. Place in a greased bowl. Cover and let rise in a warm place 1½ hours. Punch dough down; cover and let rise 45 minutes. Divide in half; cover and let rest 10 minutes. Flatten each ball into an oval. Fold long edges to the middle. Fold dough in half lengthwise. Holding each end, roll dough gently back and forth to lengthen loaf and taper ends. Place diagonally on a baking sheet that has been lightly greased and sprinkled with cornmeal. Make ¼-inch slashes in dough at 2-inch intervals, or 1 slash lengthwise. Cover and let rise in a warm place 45 to 50 minutes. Brush top with egg wash. Place in a 400° oven 40 to 45 minutes. Brush again with egg wash 10 minutes before removing from oven. Makes 2 loaves.

It's said bread is to Frenchmen what potatoes are to Germans. The typical loaf of French bread is a three to four-foot long pole-like loaf which the people carry home from the bakery under their arm.

BOHEMIAN BREAD

5 to 5½ c. Bohemian-style rye and
  wheat flour
2 pkgs. dry yeast
2 c. milk
¼ c. butter
3 T. sugar
4 t. salt
⅓ c. dark molasses

In a large mixing bowl, combine 2 cups flour and yeast. In a 1-quart saucepan, combine milk, butter, sugar and salt; heat until warm. Stir in molasses and add to flour mixture. Beat ½ minute at low speed, scraping bowl constantly, then 3 more minutes at high speed. Add 1 cup flour and beat 1 minute longer. Stir in enough remaining flour to make a soft dough. Turn onto a lightly floured surface; knead 5 to 10 minutes or until smooth and satiny. Place in a buttered bowl, turning once to butter top. Cover bowl and let rise on a rack over hot water until doubled in bulk, about 1 hour. Punch dough down and divide in half. On a lightly floured surface, roll each half into a 9 x 12-inch rectangle. Beginning with the 9-inch edge, roll dough tightly; seal final seam tightly. Seal ends of loaf and fold ends under; place in two 9 x 5 x 3-inch buttered loaf pans, seam down. Cover and allow to stand in warm place until doubled in bulk, about 1 hour. Bake in a 375° oven, 30 to 35 minutes or until loaf sounds hollow when tapped. Turn out of pans onto a wire rack to cool. Makes 2 loaves.

GOLDEN PORTUGUESE RAISIN BREAD

2 pkgs. dry yeast
1 c. sugar
1 T. salt
1 T. lemon peel
4 to 4½ c. flour
½ c. warm water
½ c. milk
½ c. butter or margarine
4 eggs
1 c. raisins

In a large bowl, mix dry yeast with sugar, salt, lemon peel and 1 cup flour. In a saucepan heat water, milk and butter until very warm (120 to 130°). Add liquid to dry ingredients and beat until smooth. Add 3 of the eggs. Mix remaining flour with raisins and add to yeast mixture. Turn out on a floured board and knead until mixture is smooth and elastic, using only enough flour to prevent sticking. Shape into a ball, place in a greased bowl and cover. Let rise in warm place until doubled in bulk. Punch down. Shape into 2 balls and place into two 9-inch greased casseroles or skillets. Cover and let rise again until doubled. Beat remaining egg and brush tops of bread. Bake in a 350° oven 30 minutes until rich golden brown. Cool before slicing. Makes 2 loaves.

KULICH
(Russian Easter Cake)

1½ c. milk, scalded
5½ to 6 c. flour
1 pkg. dry yeast
¼ c. warm water
4 egg yolks
⅔ c. sugar
¼ c. lemon-flavored instant tea
1 t. water
1 c. melted butter or margarine
⅔ c. chopped blanched almonds
⅓ c. grated lemon rind
¼ t. salt
  Pinch saffron
⅓ c. seedless golden raisins
2 46-oz. juice cans

In a large bowl, combine cooled milk and 4 cups flour. Dissolve yeast in water; then stir into the flour mixture. Cover and let rise in warm place until doubled in bulk. In small bowl, beat egg yolks with sugar until light and thick; blend in tea and 1 teaspoon water; stir into dough. Add butter and blend well. Stir in nuts, lemon rind, salt, saffron and raisins. Gradually stir in enough flour to make dough firm enough to handle; turn out on floured board and knead until smooth and elastic, working in more flour as needed. Divide dough in half and place in juice cans which have been lined with greased brown paper. Cover and let rise in warm place until doubled in bulk. Bake in a 375° oven about 1¼ hour until golden brown. Allow to cool 5 minutes; then turn out on rack to cool. When cool, stand bread upright and spread tops with White Lemon Glaze, allowing it to drizzle down the sides. Makes 2 tall loaves.

WHITE LEMON GLAZE

½ c. confectioners' sugar
2 t. hot water
1 t. lemon juice

In a small bowl, combine sugar, water and lemon juice. Blend well.

sweet yeast breads

BASIC SWEET DOUGH

- 2 cakes compressed yeast *or*
  2 pkgs. dry yeast
- 2 c. milk, scalded and cooled
- ½ c. sugar
- 2 t. salt
- 2 eggs, beaten
- 7 to 7½ c. flour
- ½ c. butter, melted and cooled

Crumble or sprinkle yeast in mixing bowl. Combine cooled milk, sugar and salt; add to yeast and stir. Let stand about 5 minutes. Add beaten eggs and half of the flour; beat until almost smooth and elastic. Add melted butter and continue to beat. Gradually add remaining flour until the dough forms a ball. Turn dough onto lightly floured board; cover and let stand 10 minutes. Then knead until smooth and elastic. Put into a greased bowl, turning to grease all sides. Cover and let rise until doubled in bulk, about 2 hours. Punch down. Let rise again until almost doubled, about 45 minutes. Punch down again and turn onto floured surface. Divide into desired portions. Let rest 15 minutes before shaping into desired rolls or coffee cakes. Makes 2 or 3 coffee cakes (8 to 9-inches round or square) or 3½ to 4 dozen rolls.

CINNAMON ROLLS

- ¼ c. melted butter
- ½ c. sugar
- 1 t. cinnamon
- ½ c. raisins

Roll out half of Basic Sweet Dough to a 20 x 10-inch rectangle. Brush with melted butter and sprinkle with sugar, cinnamon and raisins. Roll up like a jelly roll, starting at long side. Pinch edges to seal. Cut in 1-inch slices with knife or by sliding string under roll, holding one end with each hand. Pull ends together at top of roll to cut a slice. Place slices, cut side down in greased 8 or 9-inch square pan. Brush again with melted butter. Let rise until doubled. Bake in a 375° oven, about 15 to 20 minutes or until lightly browned. Remove from oven and cool. Serve plain or frost with Confectioners' Sugar Frosting (page 28). Makes about 1½ dozen rolls.

HUNGARIAN COFFEE CAKE

- 1 c. sugar
- 1 t. cinnamon
- ½ c. finely chopped walnuts
- ½ c. melted butter

Use Basic Sweet Dough recipe. Cut dough in walnut-size pieces and form into balls. Combine sugar, cinnamon and nuts. Roll each ball in melted butter, then in sugar mixture. Layer balls in 2 greased 10-inch tube cake pans or ring molds. Cover and let rise until doubled in bulk, about 45 minutes. Bake in a 350° oven 45 minutes. To remove, allow inverted pan to remain over coffee cake a few minutes to permit sugar mixture to run over cake. Break apart with two forks to serve. Makes 2 coffee cakes.

FRUIT BRAID

Roll out half of Basic Sweet Dough to a 15 x 8-inch rectangle. Spread Prune Filling or your favorite cake and pastry filling down center third of rectangle. Cut 15 strips, 1-inch wide, along each side of filling. Fold strips over each other at an angle across filling, alternating from side to side like a braid. Place on greased baking sheet. Let rise until doubled in bulk. Bake in a 375° oven about 15 to 20 minutes or until lightly browned. Remove from oven; cool on wire rack. Frost with Confectioners' Sugar Icing (page 28). Makes 1 braid.

PRUNE FILLING

- 2 c. cooked, chopped prunes
- 3 T. sugar
- 3 T. lemon juice
- 1 t. grated lemon rind

Combine all ingredients; mix well.

50

Pictured Opposite:
Irish Soda Bread, p. 48

doughnuts and fritters

CHOCOLATE DOUGHNUTS

3¾ c. flour
6 T. cocoa
1 t. salt
4 t. baking powder
½ t. cinnamon
2 T. butter
1 c. sugar
2 eggs
1 c. milk
1 t. vanilla

Sift together all dry ingredients. Cream butter; gradually add sugar and continue beating until light and fluffy. Add eggs, one at a time, beating after each addition. Add milk, vanilla, and flour mixture alternately, stirring until blended. Roll out on lightly floured board to a ½-inch thickness. Cut with floured doughnut cutter and let stand uncovered for 20 minutes. Drop into hot deep fat (365° to 375°) and fry 3 to 5 minutes or until brown, turning the doughnuts as they rise to the surface. Drain on absorbent paper. Makes about 2 dozen chocolate doughnuts.

AUNT JEAN'S RAISED DOUGHNUTS

¾ c. milk
¼ c. sugar
1 t. salt
¼ c. butter or margarine
¼ c. warm water
1 pkg. dry yeast or 1 cake compressed yeast
1 egg, beaten
3¼ c. flour
Shortening for frying

Scald milk; stir in sugar, salt and butter. Cool to lukewarm. Measure warm water into warm, large mixing bowl. Sprinkle or crumble yeast; stir until dissolved. Add lukewarm milk mixture, egg and half the flour. Beat until smooth. Stir in enough additional flour to make a soft dough. Turn dough out onto lightly floured board. Knead until smooth and elastic, about 10 minutes.

Place in a greased bowl, turning to grease all sides. Cover and let rise in warm place until doubled in bulk, about 1 hour. Punch dough down. Roll out about ½ inch thick. Cut with a 2½-inch doughnut cutter. Place on greased baking sheets. Cover and let rise in warm place until doubled in bulk, about 1 hour. Handle doughnuts as little as possible to prevent falling. Fry in deep fat (375°) for 2 to 3 minutes or until brown on both sides. Drain on absorbent paper. While warm, dip in Doughnut Glaze or cinnamon-sugar. Makes about 20 doughnuts.

DOUGHNUT GLAZE

2 c. confectioners' sugar
⅓ c. milk
1 t. vanilla

Blend confectioners' sugar, milk and vanilla. Dip warm doughnuts into glaze. Drain on rack set over waxed paper or platter to catch icing so it may be reused.

APPLESAUCE DOUGHNUT PUFFS

2¼ c. flour
2 t. baking powder
1 t. baking soda
1 t. allspice
¼ t. salt
2 eggs
1 c. brown sugar, firmly packed
1 T. salad oil
1 8½-oz. can applesauce
¼ c. milk
Salad oil for frying
Granulated sugar

Sift together flour, baking powder, baking soda, allspice and salt. Beat eggs; gradually beat in brown sugar and oil. Mix in applesauce. Add dry ingredients alternately with milk, mixing well after each addition. Drop by teaspoonfuls into hot oil (370°). Fry until golden brown on both sides. Drain; roll in sugar. Makes about 4 dozen puffs.

BISMARKS

1⅔ c. milk
1 pkg. dry yeast
¼ c. lukewarm water
8 egg yolks
½ c. sugar
5¼ c. flour
1 t. salt
Melted butter
Jelly
Confectioners' sugar
Granulated sugar

Scald milk and cool to lukewarm. Dissolve yeast in lukewarm water. Beat egg yolks until thick and lemon colored. Add sugar gradually, beating well after each addition. Add dissolved yeast and the cooled milk to egg yolk-sugar mixture. Mix well. Add flour and salt; beat until dough is smooth. Place in greased bowl, brush top with melted butter and cover. Let rise in warm place until double. Punch down. Turn out on a floured surface. Dough will be sticky. Use plenty of flour on hands. Divide dough in half. Shape each half into a round ball. Roll one-half on floured board to ¼-inch thickness. Cut rounds with a biscuit cutter. Drop jelly in center of half of the rounds. Top with the other plain rounds. Recut, using slightly smaller cutter. This seals edges and holds in the jelly. Repeat with second ball of dough. Place 2 inches apart on floured surface; cover and let rise in warm place until doubled. Fry in deep fat (365°) until golden brown on both sides. Remove and drain. Serve plain or sprinkle with confectioners' or granulated sugar. Makes about 3 dozen Bismarks.

PUFFY CORN FRITTERS

1⅓ c. flour
1½ t. baking powder
¾ t. salt
1 T. sugar
⅔ c. milk
1 egg, well beaten
1 1-lb. 1-oz. can whole kernel corn, drained
Deep fat

Sift together first 4 ingredients. Blend milk with egg; add gradually to dry ingredients. Stir in corn and drop from tablespoons into deep hot fat, (375°); fry until golden brown, about 4 to 8 minutes, depending upon size. Drain on absorbent paper and serve with maple syrup. Makes 16 to 20 fritters.

FRUITED DOUGHNUTS

2 pkgs. dry yeast
4½ c. sifted flour
½ c. lukewarm water
½ c. butter, softened
⅓ c. sugar
½ t. salt
1 t. grated lemon peel
2 eggs, beaten
½ c. lukewarm milk
½ c. golden raisins
½ c. mixed candied fruit
Deep fat
Confectioners' sugar

Sprinkle dry yeast over ½ cup sifted flour; pour lukewarm water over and stir until blended. Set aside in a warm place for 20 minutes. Cream butter with sugar. Gradually add salt, lemon peel, eggs and milk. Add yeast mixture. Stir 2 cups flour into butter-yeast mixture; knead in remaining flour by hand, then raisins and fruit. Roll dough to a ½-inch thickness and cut doughnuts. Place on floured board and let rise until doubled in size. Fry in deep fat (350° to 400°) turning to brown both sides. Dust with confectioners' sugar. Makes 2 dozen doughnuts.

OATMEAL DOUGHNUT DROPS

2 c. milk
¼ c. butter or margarine
⅔ c. brown sugar, firmly packed
2 t. salt
1½ c. flour
2 eggs
1 t. cinnamon
¼ t. nutmeg
¼ t. cloves
2 pkgs. dry yeast
2 c. whole wheat flour
1 c. rolled oats
Deep fat
Granulated sugar

Heat milk, butter, brown sugar and salt to scalding. Cool to lukewarm. Pour into large bowl of mixer. Add 1 cup of the flour; beat 2 minutes. Add eggs, one at a time, beating constantly. Add cinnamon, nutmeg and cloves. Add the remaining ½ cup of flour and the yeast. Beat an additional 2 minutes. Stir in whole wheat flour and oats; cover and refrigerate 2 to 48 hours. Stir dough down. Drop by rounded teaspoons into hot deep fat (375°); cook until well browned on both sides. Drain on absorbent paper. Coat with sugar; serve warm. Makes about 8 dozen.

BANANA FRITTERS

¾ c. flour
3 T. sugar
⅛ t. cinnamon
½ t. baking powder
2 eggs
½ c. milk
¾ c. mashed ripe banana
½ t. vanilla
    Salad oil

In a large bowl, mix flour, sugar, cinnamon and baking powder. In another bowl, beat together eggs, milk, mashed banana and vanilla. Stir liquid ingredients all at once into flour mixture, stirring until smooth. Let batter rest 30 minutes. Pour oil into a large saucepan to half full and heat over medium heat to 350°. Drop batter by tablespoons into hot oil. Cook 5 minutes or until golden brown. Repeat with remaining batter. Keep warm in a 250° oven. To serve, sprinkle with confectioners' sugar. Makes 20 fritters.

CHOCOLATE DOUGHNUT PUFFS

2 T. cream
    Buttermilk
2 eggs
1 c. sugar
2 1-oz. squares baking chocolate
1 T. butter
3¼ c. flour
½ t. salt
¼ t. nutmeg
2 t. baking powder
1 t. baking soda
1 t. vanilla
    Confectioners' sugar

Add enough buttermilk to cream to make 1 cup. Set aside. Beat eggs with sugar. Melt baking chocolate with butter; cool. Sift together flour, salt, nutmeg, baking powder and soda. Add flour and liquid alternately (about half of it) to the egg mixture. Add melted chocolate, then the remaining flour and liquid. Add the vanilla; blend to moisten. Drop by teaspoonfuls into hot fat (375°), by using two teaspoons, dipping the "dipping" teaspoon into the hot fat so the dough won't cling to it. Use the other teaspoon to ease the dough into the frying fat. Turn puffs as they rise to the surface. Fry until evenly browned. Drain on absorbent paper. Dust with confectioners' sugar. Makes about 4 dozen puffs.

BAKED DOUGHNUTS

4½ to 5 c. flour
2 pkgs. dry yeast
1 c. milk
¾ c. water
⅓ c. salad oil
¼ c. sugar
2 t. salt
1½ t. nutmeg
¼ t. cinnamon
2 eggs, room temperature
    Melted butter
    Orange Glaze

Stir together 2 cups flour and yeast. Heat milk, water, oil, sugar, salt and spices until very warm (120° to 130°), stirring to blend. Cool to lukewarm. Add liquid ingredients to flour-yeast mixture and beat until smooth, about 2 minutes on medium speed of electric mixer or 300 strokes by hand. Blend in eggs. Add 1 cup flour and beat 1 minute on medium speed or 150 strokes by hand. Stir in more flour to make a very thick batter. Cover and let rise in warm place until doubled, about 1 hour. Stir down dough. Turn onto a well-floured surface and turn dough over 2 or 3 times to shape into a soft ball. Roll out ½ inch thick and cut with floured doughnut cutter. Place doughnuts 2 inches apart on greased baking sheets. Brush with melted butter and let rise in warm place until doubled, about 20 minutes. Bake in a 425° oven 8 to 10 minutes. Remove from baking sheets. Dip tops in Orange Glaze while warm. Makes about 3 dozen.

ORANGE GLAZE

2 c. confectioners' sugar
¼ c. orange juice

Stir sugar and juice together until smooth.

Deep-frying is what makes a fritter a fritter. Any tasty bit of fruit, vegetable or meat, dipped in batter and fried in deep hot fat is a fritter. Plump, savory fritters are perfect complements to a slice of broiled ham; and rich, moist fruit fritters, rolled in sugar, make a tempting dessert.

pancakes and waffles

BUTTERMILK PANCAKES

2 eggs
2½ c. buttermilk
2½ c. flour
1 t. baking soda
2 t. baking powder
1 t. salt
2 T. sugar
¼ c. melted butter

Beat eggs; add buttermilk. Sift and add flour, soda, baking powder, salt and sugar, blending well. Add melted butter; mix well. Drop from spoon on lightly greased griddle and brown on both sides until done. Makes 20 to 24 medium-size pancakes.

AEBLESKIVER
(Danish Pancakes)

2 c. milk
3 eggs, separated
2 c. flour
1 t. salt
4 t. baking powder
1 T. sugar
Vegetable oil

Combine milk and egg yolks. Sift together dry ingredients and add to milk and egg mixture. Beat egg whites until stiff. Fold in. Heat aebleskiver pan. Put about 1 teaspoon of vegetable oil in each cup of the aebleskiver pan. Put enough batter in each cup to almost fill it. Use metal knitting needle to turn aebleskivers. Keep turning them until golden brown. Add additional shortening for each frying. Serve with syrup, jams or jellies. Makes about 3 dozen aebleskivers.

The griddle is the right temperature for pancakes when a few drops of water dropped on it, form little beads that dance on the surface.

BLUEBERRY WAFFLES

1⅓ c. flour
2 T. sugar
2½ t. baking powder
½ t. salt
2 eggs, separated
1 c. milk
⅓ c. melted shortening
1 c. blueberries, rinsed and drained

Combine flour, sugar, baking powder and salt. Stir well to blend. Stir in egg yolks and milk; add shortening, mixing well. Add blueberries and blend well. Beat egg whites until stiff peaks form; fold into mixture. Bake on a preheated waffle iron until golden brown. Makes four 9-inch square waffles.

PUMPKIN PUFF PANCAKES

2 eggs
1 c. milk
½ c. cooked pumpkin
1¾ c. buttermilk baking mix
2 T. sugar
½ t. cinnamon
½ t. nutmeg
½ t. ginger
¼ c. salad oil

In small mixer bowl, beat eggs on high speed 5 minutes or until thick and lemon colored. Stir in remaining ingredients. Drop batter by tablespoonfuls onto medium-hot ungreased griddle. Bake until puffed and bubbles break. Turn and bake other side until golden brown. Makes about 5 dozen 2-inch pancakes.

MAPLE RUM-FLAVORED SYRUP

1 c. maple-flavored syrup
1 T. butter or margarine
½ t. rum flavoring

Heat syrup and butter or margarine. Remove from heat and stir in rum flavoring. Serve warm. Makes about 1 cup.

BUCKWHEAT PANCAKES

- 1 pkg. dry yeast
- ½ c. warm water
- 2 c. cold water
- 1 c. flour
- 2 c. buckwheat flour
- 1½ t. salt
- 1 t. baking soda
- ½ c. hot water
- 1 T. molasses
- ¼ c. melted butter

Dissolve yeast in warm water; add cold water. Sift together flour, buckwheat flour and salt; stir into yeast mixture. Beat vigorously until smooth. Cover and place in refrigerator overnight. In the morning, dissolve soda in hot water. Stir molasses, butter and soda water into dough. Let stand at room temperature 30 minutes. Pour batter from spoon onto griddle, turning when pancakes are puffed and bubbly. Makes 3 dozen 4-inch pancakes.

PEANUT WAFFLES

- 2 c. sifted flour
- 1 T. baking powder
- ½ t. salt
- 1 T. sugar
- 3 eggs, separated
- 1¼ c. milk
- ¼ c. peanut oil
- ¾ c. chopped salted peanuts

Sift together flour, baking powder, salt, and sugar. Beat egg yolks, beat in milk and add to dry ingredients. Stir in peanut oil, stirring until smooth. Beat egg whites until stiff and fold into batter. Fold in peanuts and bake on a hot waffle iron until steaming stops. Serve at once with butter and Orange Sugar. Makes 4 to 6 servings.

ORANGE SUGAR

Blend 1 teaspoon grated orange rind with ½ cup sugar until evenly mixed.

CHOCOLATE-PEANUT DESSERT WAFFLES

Use recipe for Peanut Waffles, substituting ¾ cup chopped chocolate-covered peanuts for salted peanuts. Serve warm with ice cream and chocolate sauce.

Cooking with natural foods is not new in country kitchens. For as far back as we care to count, our ancestors used honey as a natural sweetener. Almost every civilization has valued honey as food, medicine and trading commodity. Romans paid their taxes with it and many an ancient Greek and Roman chef became famous for his honey recipes.

NATURAL SYRUPS

Natural syrups include honey, molasses, and maple syrup. Mix honey and butter together or add cinnamon to the mixture to taste.

FRUIT SAUCE

Sweeten favorite berries or peaches and let steep in their own juices. Fill each pancake with the fruit mixture, roll up, and sprinkle with confectioners' sugar or serve with whipped cream.

CORNY CAKES

- 1 c. cornflake crumbs
- 1 c. flour
- 4 t. baking powder
- ½ t. salt
- 1 T. sugar
- 2 eggs
- ¼ c. vegetable oil
- 2 c. milk

In small mixing bowl, combine cornflake crumbs, flour, baking powder, salt and sugar. Mix well and set aside. In large bowl, beat eggs until foamy. Stir in vegetable oil and milk. Add dry ingredients and mix until batter is smooth. Let stand about 2 minutes. Cook about ¼ cup per each cake on a greased and preheated griddle, turning once, until golden brown on both sides. Serve hot with Pineapple Sauce. Makes about 14 pancakes.

PINEAPPLE SAUCE

- ½ c. brown sugar, firmly packed
- 1 T. cornstarch
- 2 T. butter
- 2½ c. undrained crushed pineapple
- ½ lb. Canadian bacon, cubed

Measure brown sugar and cornstarch into a medium-size saucepan; stir to combine. Add butter, pineapple and Canadian bacon. Cook over low heat, stirring frequently, until bubbly and thickened. Serve warm. Makes 3 cups.

holiday breads

HOT-CROSS BUNS

    2 c. milk, scalded
    1 c. butter
    1 c. sugar
    2 cakes yeast
    ⅓ c. lukewarm water
    2 eggs
    8 c. flour
    1 t. salt
    1½ c. raisins
    1 t. cinnamon or nutmeg

Pour scalded milk over butter and sugar, stirring to dissolve. Cool to lukewarm. Dissolve yeast in lukewarm water. Stir yeast and eggs into milk mixture. Dust raisins with a small amount of the flour; stir in remaining flour and salt. Add spice and floured raisins and knead in thoroughly. Place in a buttered bowl, cover and let rise until doubled in bulk. Punch dough down and turn out onto a floured board. Shape into 30 buns and place on buttered cookie sheets. Cover and let rise for 30 minutes; carefully press the shape of a cross into each bun, using a spatula or the back of a knife. Bake in a 375° oven 10 minutes. Reduce heat to 350° and continue baking until buns are browned, about 10 to 15 minutes longer. Frost either the entire bun or just the shape of the cross with White Frosting. Makes 30 buns.

WHITE FROSTING

1 egg white
1 t. lemon juice, vanilla or almond extract
   Confectioners' sugar

Beat egg white until stiff. Gradually add enough confectioners' sugar to make mixture thick. Add flavoring. If frosting is too thin, add more confectioners' sugar.

The breads of Easter are special breads—rich and delectable as the signs of spring itself. Easter breads traditionally marked the end of Lenten fasting. A special part of our rich heritage, their fragrance has filled country kitchens for generations.

Pictured Opposite:
Corny Cakes, p. 57

EASTER EGG BREAD

    12 eggs, in shell
       Egg coloring
    ½ c. milk, scalded
    ½ c. sugar
    1 t. salt
    ½ c. butter
       Grated rinds of 2 lemons
    2 pkgs. dry yeast
    ½ c. warm water
    2 eggs, slightly beaten
    4½ c. flour
    1 egg, beaten
       Tiny decorating candies

Wash eggs, tint shells with egg coloring and set aside. Add sugar, salt, butter and lemon rind to scalded milk. Cool to lukewarm. Dissolve yeast in warm water; add to milk mixture with eggs and 2½ cups flour. Beat until smooth. Stir in enough remaining flour, a little at a time, to form a dough that is easy to handle. Turn onto a lightly floured board and knead until smooth and elastic, 5 to 8 minutes. Place in lightly greased bowl, turning to grease top. Cover and let rise in warm place until doubled in bulk. Punch down, let rise again. Divide into 4 parts. Form each part into a 36-inch rope. On a greased baking sheet shape 2 of the ropes into a very loosely braided ring, leaving space for 6 eggs. Repeat with other ropes of dough for second ring. Insert colored eggs in each ring. Cover and let rise until doubled in bulk. Brush with beaten egg. Sprinkle with decorating candies. Bake in a 375° oven 20 minutes or until lightly browned. Serve warm. Makes 2 large rings.

FROSTED EASTER EGG ROLLS

Thaw a one-pound loaf of frozen cinnamon or raisin bread dough, and allow to rise until doubled in size. Break off pieces of dough and roll into the shape of an egg. Place "eggs" in a lightly greased pie pan and bake in a 350° oven until lightly browned, about 25 minutes. Cool on a wire rack. When cool, decorate eggs with colored frostings.

WALNUT KOLACHE

1 cake yeast
¼ c. warm water
¾ c. milk
¼ c. shortening
3 T. sugar
1½ t. salt
1 egg, beaten
3 c. flour
¾ c. walnuts, chopped
Melted butter
12 dried apricots or prunes, cooked
Glaze

Soften yeast in warm water and set aside. Scald milk; add shortening, sugar and salt until shortening melts and sugar dissolves. Cool to lukewarm. Add egg and dissolved yeast. Stir in half the flour and beat until smooth. Add ½ cup walnuts, then gradually blend in remaining flour. Drop by heaping tablespoonfuls onto lightly greased baking sheets. Brush with butter. Let rise until doubled, about 1 hour. Dip apricots or prunes into remaining ¼ cup walnuts and press one into center of each roll. Bake in a 350° oven for about 25 minutes, until nicely browned. While still warm, spread with Glaze. Makes 1 dozen Kolache.

GLAZE

1 c. confectioners' sugar
1 T. hot water
¼ t. vanilla

Combine all ingredients, stirring until smooth.

HOLIDAY HORNS

5 to 5½ c. flour
2 pkgs. dry yeast
½ c. milk
½ c. water
½ c. sugar
¼ c. vegetable oil
2½ t. salt
2 eggs
1 c. finely chopped walnuts
1 6-oz. pkg. semisweet chocolate chips
1 c. chopped maraschino cherries
Vegetable oil
Cinnamon-sugar, if desired

Stir together 2 cups flour and yeast. Combine milk, water, sugar, ¼ cup oil and salt and heat over low heat until warm, stirring to blend. Add liquid ingredients to flour-yeast mixture and beat until smooth, about 2 minutes on medium speed of electric mixer. Blend in eggs. Add 1 cup flour and beat 1 minute on medium speed. Stir in more flour to make a moderately stiff dough. Turn onto a lightly floured surface and knead until smooth and satiny, about 8 to 10 minutes. Shape into a ball and place in a lightly greased bowl, turning to grease all sides. Cover and let rise in warm place until doubled, about 1½ hours. Punch dough down; divide in half. Cover and let rest 10 minutes. Roll each half to a 15-inch circle. Combine nuts, chocolate and cherries; sprinkle half over each circle, pressing gently into dough. Cut each circle into 16 wedges. Roll up each wedge, beginning at wide end. Place on greased baking sheet with points underneath. Brush with oil and sprinkle with cinnamon-sugar, if desired. Let rise in a warm place until doubled in bulk, about 30 minutes. Bake in a 350° oven 20 to 25 minutes. Serve warm. Makes 32 sweet rolls.

MOTHER D'S YULE LOAF

1 pkg. dry yeast
½ c. lukewarm water
1 c. milk, scalded and cooled
¼ c. sugar
⅓ c. butter
2 t. salt
4 to 4½ c. flour
1 egg, beaten
1 c. rolled oats, uncooked
1 c. mixed candied fruit
½ c. chopped walnuts

Soften yeast in lukewarm water. Combine scalded milk with sugar, butter, and salt. Set aside to cool to lukewarm. Beat in 1½ cups flour. Add beaten egg and softened yeast. Stir in rolled oats, candied fruit and nuts. Stir in enough additional flour to make a soft dough. Turn out on lightly floured surface and knead until smooth and satiny, about 10 minutes. Place dough in greased bowl, turning once to grease surface. Cover and let rise in a warm place until doubled in bulk, about 1¾ hours. Punch down, cover and let rest 10 minutes. Shape dough into 2 round loaves. Place on greased baking sheets. Cover and let rise until dough is doubled in bulk, about 1 hour. Bake in a 375° oven 30 minutes or until lightly browned. Cool and frost with confectioners' frosting. Decorate with additional candied fruit and nuts. Makes 2 round loaves.

HUTZELBROT
(German Christmas Fruit Bread)

6½ c. flour, divided
2 pkgs. dry yeast
⅓ c. sugar
2 t. ground cinnamon
1 t. salt
1 t. ground anise seed
½ t. ground cloves
1½ c. water
1 c. milk
¼ c. butter or margarine
1 14-oz. pkg. figs, chopped
1 12-oz. pkg. pitted prunes, chopped
1 10-oz. pkg. pitted dates, chopped
1 c. diced dried pears or apples
1 c. coarsely chopped walnuts
½ c. diced candied orange peel

In a large bowl of electric mixer, combine 2½ cups of the flour, yeast, sugar, cinnamon, salt, anise and cloves. Set aside. In a medium saucepan, combine water, milk and butter. Heat slowly until lukewarm (butter does not need to melt). Add to flour mixture and beat at low speed until blended. Beat at high speed for 3 minutes. With a wooden spoon, stir in remaining ingredients and mix well. Stir in enough flour (about 2½ cups) to make a soft dough. Turn out onto a lightly floured board; knead in enough flour (about 1½ cups) to make a smooth dough. Place in a lightly greased bowl; turn dough so that greased side is up. Cover lightly with a towel and let rise in a warm place until doubled in bulk, about 1½ hours. Punch dough down. Cut into 2 equal parts; shape each part into an oval and place on lightly greased baking sheets. Cover lightly; let rise in a warm place until doubled in bulk, about 1 hour. Bake in a 375° oven until golden and bread sounds hollow when tapped with fingers, about 35 minutes. Remove bread to wire racks and cool. Makes 2 loaves.

CHRISTMAS TREE COFFEE CAKE

4½ to 5 c. flour
2 pkgs. dry yeast
1¼ c. milk
½ c. butter
¼ c. sugar
1 t. salt
2 t. grated orange peel
2 eggs
1 egg yolk

In a large mixing bowl combine 2 cups flour and yeast. In a 1-quart saucepan combine milk, butter, sugar and salt; heat until very warm and add orange peel. Add liquid to flour. Add eggs and egg yolk. Beat ½ minute at low speed, scraping bowl constantly; then 3 more minutes at high speed. Add 1 cup flour and beat 1 minute longer. Stir in enough remaining flour to form a soft dough (about 1¼ to 1½ cups). Turn onto lightly floured surface; knead 5 to 10 minutes or until dough is smooth and satiny. Add only enough more flour to keep dough from sticking to the board. Place in buttered bowl, turning once to butter top. Cover bowl with waxed paper and towel and let stand in a warm place until doubled in bulk, about 1 to 1½ hours. Prepare Filling. Punch dough down and turn onto a lightly floured surface; cover with towel and let rest 10 minutes. Roll dough out to form a 16 x 14-inch rectangle. Cut off a strip 14 x 2 inches; set aside for trim. Spread Filling on square of dough. Fold dough in thirds. Roll out to make a 14 x 9-inch rectangle. Cut off a strip 9 x 2-inches, divide this strip in half and set aside to use as bases for trees. From the long side of dough, cut a triangle from top edge center point to bottom outside edges. Place on a cookie sheet; place two remaining half trees on another cookie sheet, straight sides together. Pinch center seam to seal. Place bases at bottom of tree and pinch to seal. Decorate trees with remaining dough, making ropes or ornaments. To make ornaments wrap small balls of dough around red or green candied cherries. (Brush dough with a little water so decorations will stick.) Brush melted butter over trees. Cover with waxed paper, then a towel. Let rise in a warm place until doubled in bulk, about 40 minutes. Bake in a 350° oven 15 to 20 minutes. Carefully slide onto wire racks to cool. Decorate before serving. Use a pastry brush to brush on icing. Makes 2 coffee cakes.

FILLING

1 8-oz. can almond paste
½ c. finely chopped almonds
¼ c. butter, softened
1 egg white

Blend together almond paste, almonds, butter and egg white.

ICING

1¼ c. confectioners' sugar
2 to 3 T. milk
½ t. vanilla

Combine sugar and milk, mix until smooth, add vanilla.

GUMDROP BATTER BREAD

3 to 3¼ c. flour
1 pkg. dry yeast
½ t. cinnamon
¼ t. nutmeg
½ c. milk
½ c. water
½ c. vegetable oil
¼ c. sugar
1 t. salt
2 eggs
1½ c. chopped spice-flavored gumdrops
Glaze

Stir together 1½ cups flour, yeast, cinnamon and nutmeg. In a saucepan, combine milk, water, oil, sugar and salt. Heat slowly until warm, stirring to blend. Add liquid ingredients to flour-yeast mixture and beat until smooth, about 2 minutes on medium speed of electric mixer. Blend in eggs and gumdrops. Stir in more flour to make stiff batter. Beat until batter is elastic, about 1 minute on medium speed. Divide batter into two well-greased, 1-quart baking dishes or molds. Let rise in a warm place until light and bubbly, about 1 hour. Bake in a 375° oven 30 to 35 minutes. Cool 10 minutes before removing from dish or mold. Cool completely. Frost with Glaze and decorate if desired. Makes 2 loaves.

GLAZE

1 c. confectioners' sugar
1 T. milk

Blend ingredients until smooth and of spreading consistency.

HUNGARIAN BUTTERHORNS

1 pkg. dry yeast
1 t. sugar
½ t. salt
1½ c. butter
4 eggs, separated
1 c. sour cream
4 c. flour
1 c. confectioners' sugar
¾ c. finely ground walnuts
Confectioners' Sugar Frosting
Nuts

Combine yeast with sugar and salt; mix and set aside. Cream butter until soft and fluffy; add egg yolks, sour cream and yeast mixture. Cream well. Add flour and blend well. Divide dough into 6 rolls and place in refrigerator to chill at least 1 hour or overnight. When ready to work, beat egg whites until stiff, beat in 1 cup confectioners' sugar; fold in ground nuts. Set aside. Work with only one portion of dough at a time and roll out on a confectioners' sugared surface. Spread with egg white mixture. Cut into wedges; roll up each wedge, starting at wide end. Place on a lightly greased baking sheet. Bake in a 375° oven, 20 minutes. Frost with Confectioners' Sugar Frosting (page 28) while warm and sprinkle with nuts. Makes 6 dozen.

STOLLEN

1 pkg. dry yeast
¼ c. warm water
1 c. milk, scalded
½ c. sugar
½ c. butter or margarine, softened
1 t. salt
¼ t. ground cardamom
4½ to 5 c. sifted flour
2 eggs, beaten
1 c. golden seedless raisins
1 c. chopped mixed candied fruit
½ c. chopped almonds
1 T. brandy
1 T. grated lemon rind
1½ c. sifted confectioners' sugar
2 T. hot water
⅛ t. almond extract

Soften yeast in warm water. Combine scalded milk, sugar, butter, salt and cardamom and cool to lukewarm. Stir in 2 cups flour. Add eggs, mixing well. Stir in softened yeast, raisins, candied fruit, almonds, brandy and lemon rind. Add remaining flour to make a soft dough; mix well. Turn out on a lightly floured board and knead until smooth and elastic, about 8 minutes. Place in lightly greased bowl, turning once to grease surface. Cover and let rise in warm place until doubled in bulk, about 2 hours. Punch dough down and divide into two balls. Cover and let rest for 10 minutes. Lightly roll each into a 10 x 6-inch oval. Fold each oval lengthwise to within 1 inch of the opposite side. Cover and let rise on greased baking sheet in warm place until doubled. Bake in a 350° oven, 25 to 30 minutes. Combine confectioners' sugar, water and almond extract; mix well. While bread is warm, spread with sugar glaze. Makes 2 loaves.

index

At one time the first loaf of bread made from the year's last sheaf of wheat was highly prized by early man. He believed it to possess a magic quality protecting him from ill health and misfortune.

A very special thank you to the following for their cooperation and help in supplying selected recipes from their test kitchens and files: Alabama Peanut Producers Association, American Spice Trade Association, Banana Bunch, Best Foods, California Apricot Advisory Board, California Honey Advisory Board, California Plum Commodity Committee, California Raisin Advisory Board, Del Monte Corporation, Diamond Walnut Growers, Inc., Florida Citrus Commission, General Foods Consumer Center, General Mills, Inc., Glidden-Durkee, Gold Meadow Dairies, Grandma's Molasses, International Multifoods, Kellogg Company, Libby, McNeill & Libby, National Kraut Packers Association, Nordic Ware, Oklahoma Peanut Commission, Pillsbury Company, Potato Board, Quaker Oats Company, R. T. French Company, San Luis Valley Potato Administrative Committee, Stokely-Van Camp, Inc., Sunkist Growers, Inc., Sunsweet Growers, Inc., United Dairy Industry Association, Wheat Flour Institute.

C 2
D 3
E 4
F 5
G 6
H 7
I 8
K 9
L 0
M 1